Verdi

Verdi

Barbara Meier

translated by Rosemary Smith
introduced by Roger Parker

HAUS PUBLISHING · LONDON

First published in German in the Rowohlt monographien series
© 2000 Rowolht Taschenbuch Verlag GmbH

This English translation first published in Great Britain in 2003 by
Haus Publishing Limited
32 Store Street
London WC1E 7BS

English translation © Rosemary Smith, 2003
Introduction © Roger Parker, 2003

The moral right of the authors has been asserted

A CIP catalogue record for this book
is available from the British Library

ISBN 1-904341-05-5 (paperback)
ISBN 1-904341-04-7 (hardback)

Designed and typeset in Albertina at Libanus Press, Marlborough

Printed and bound by Graphicom in Vicenza, Italy

Front cover: painting of Giuseppe Verdi by Boldoni
courtesy of Mary Evans Picture Library
Back cover: caricature by Verdi courtesy of the Lebrecht Music Collection

Contents

Introduction

Although Verdi died more than 100 years ago, his star has never been higher in the operatic skies. His operas are at the centre of the repertory, and the huge centenary celebrations of 2001 merely underlined that fact: it is almost inevitable that every one of his 27 operas will have been staged somewhere in the world during the last year, quite a few of them in some unusual version to give them added cachet or novelty. Verdi continues to engage us with uncommon intensity: he continues to be basic to our sense of what constitutes musical drama.

This extraordinary state of affairs would have been unthinkable only a couple of generations ago, perhaps particularly in Britain. Not long in the past, only about eight of his most popular operas remained stubbornly in the repertory; practically everything pre-*Rigoletto* had disappeared; many of the later works were thought to be 'problem pieces'; and it was hard to find much more than amused contempt for almost all of Verdi's music among refined circles. I remember my English teacher at school in the 1960s, a committed disciple of F R Leavis and a severe arbiter of musical taste. He had travelled to London hoping to see *The Marriage of Figaro*, but had mixed up his dates and arrived at the theatre to see on the billboard those awful words TONIGHT: *RIGOLETTO*. The idea of staying to attend this farrago was, of course, 'absurd' (a favourite word of disparagement). He austerely returned home, doubtless to a soothing extract or two from Karl Böhm's *Così fan tutte* before bed.

Long before this, though, the first signs of a renewed interest in Verdi had appeared in continental Europe. The early headway was made in Germany during the 1920s and 1930s. There were many external reasons for the shift in fashion. A reaction against Wagner, both among the public and among self-styled 'modern' composers, was certainly one factor. Equally important was a prevailing sense of 'opera crisis': new operas were no longer being produced in great number, so a vogue developed for resurrecting old works, often with controversial stagings that attempted to bring them aggressively up to date. Other, partially forgotten opera composers benefited from these conditions, in particular Handel, Gluck and Mozart: but Verdi's works led the way. By the 1930s a full-scale 'Verdi renaissance' was under way. The trend continued even during the Third Reich, gaining extra fuel from the need to establish cultural levels on which the tottering Axis partnership could be seen as mutually supportive. Joseph Goebbels personally organised Verdi celebrations in both 1941 and 1943, and articles praising Verdi's 'racial and mental purity' dutifully accompanied these increasingly beleaguered wartime festivals. Answering echoes came from Italy, where the Duce promoted a number of prestigious productions and publications.

Strangely enough, though, and in marked contrast to Wagner, Verdi's association with fascism did him little harm. When Milan's La Scala re-opened after the Second World War, with Toscanini (a famous anti-fascist) conducting, they nevertheless sang Verdi: no one else seemed possible. From then onwards, with no post-war mud clinging to his boots, Verdi has marched on ever more triumphantly. The global expansion of opera in the 1980s and 1990s (the era of the 'three tenors') was spearheaded by Verdi, and more of his operas are now in the standard repertory than at any time in the past (including his own lifetime). We live, in other words, in an ever-enlarging Verdi museum. In one sense, the movement seems close to saturation point – there are simply no 'forgotten' works left to pad out our repertory. But in another, that seems to matter not at all. Verdi's operas, all of them, continue to inspire fresh interpretations, and to show a remarkable capacity (as they always did) to penetrate markedly different levels of culture. We can see *La forza del destino* in the elite splendour of the Royal Opera House; but we can then return home to hear one of its most famous melodies helping to sell beer on TV.

Not surprisingly, this explosion of interest has also stimulated writers and critics, especially over the last 30 or so years. How, then, has the Verdi critical landscape changed? How has our image of the composer altered? There are two main areas in which lines are being redrawn, both of which are reflected in the changed picture that emerges from Barbara Meier's stimulating short biography. The first concerns Verdi's reputation as a 'political' composer. The idea that Verdi's early operas heightened the Italian people's national consciousness – in extreme versions, actively led Italians to the barricades – has been a commonplace since his lifetime: indeed, some strands of the story (in particular that the Chorus of Hebrew Slaves from *Nabucco* was an unofficial hymn of the Risorgimento) were actively encouraged by Verdi himself in later life. But the most recent scholarship has found little hard evidence to support this attractive picture of the 'revolutionary' artist. The same anecdotes (of demonstrations in the theatre, of 'Viva Verdi!' shouted in the streets, etc.) are endlessly recycled; but few of them can be traced back any further than the late nineteenth century, to a time when a newly emerging Italian nation was in desperate need of 'national monuments' to bind together its fragile and fragmented people. This is not, of course, to deny the stirring force of Verdi's early music, in particular his treatment of the chorus (ie 'the people') as a dynamic new expressive power; nor indeed that he was a staunch patriot. But connections between his early music and political events were largely made some time after the revolutionary atmosphere had cooled: they have significance above all in late nineteenth-century Italy's troubled nationalism.

The second area in which signs of a new Verdi are emerging concerns his private life, although here critics are in much more difficult territory, if only because the 'evidence' is much more fragile. As Barbara Meier sensitively reveals, Verdi's carefully constructed image as a genial old man with a white beard and a battered felt hat – an image endlessly disseminated in the 2001 celebrations – has not survived critical scrutiny entirely unscathed. Looked at closely, we are aware of a dark side to his character, fuelled no doubt by a lifelong emotional insecurity. That this insecurity may well have been the key to his ability to communicate so immediately through his art is of course the constant paradox that greets those who delve into the biographies of creative minds.

An interesting example concerns the early stages of his relationship with the singer Giuseppina Strepponi, a woman who perforce claims a large place in any Verdi biography. After they first formed a partnership, she and Verdi were bold enough to live together openly, but they were in free-wheeling Paris where this was unexceptionable; after a year or so they went back to Verdi's home town, and eventually set up home in the villa and farmlands of Sant'Agata, where they would remain for the rest of their long lives. In semi-rural, priest-ridden Busseto, a couple 'living in sin' was not to be tolerated: a kind of holy war seems to have broken out. Verdi's ex-father-in-law and beloved mentor, Antonio Barezzi, was obviously caught up in the fracas, and early in 1852 Verdi sent him a famous letter, quoted by Meier:

In my house there lives a free and independent lady who loves solitude, as I do, and who has her own financial means which shelter her from need. Neither she nor I need account to anyone for our actions; and what is more, who is to know what the relationship between us may be? What business arrangements? What ties? What claims I have on her and she on me? Who knows whether she is my wife or not? And who knows what particular reasons we may have in this case for not making the matter public? Who knows if that is a good thing or a bad one? Why should it not be a good thing? And even if it were a bad one, who has the right to ostracise us? What I can say is that in my house she should be granted the same respect as I enjoy, perhaps more even, and no one should forget it, for whatever reason; and that she has a perfect right to this on account of her behaviour, her intellect, and on account of the particular consideration which she never fails to show to others (p 58).

In many ways this letter hints at the kind of man Verdi was to become in later life. It is certainly explicit, indeed full of uncompromising statements about liberty and honour and honesty; and it boldly promises to 'raise the curtain' on his private life. But behind the curtain so theatrically raised is really just another curtain, a string of rhetorical questions to which is added the deliberately misleading implication that he and Strepponi might be married after all, which they certainly were not. We can interpret this as a statement of a proud, isolated genius struggling against the petty tyrannies of provincial life – that is certainly part of the story, and has been well told. But there is also more than a hint of insecurity – of what would become in later life an occasional inability to understand that other people (people close to him) needed to lead their lives differently, and had a right to do so.

The end, though, was harrowing. Strepponi died in November 1897, carried off by pneumonia after long and painful illness, hoping in the last words of her will to be reunited with her husband in heaven. There are, after that, some very sad final letters to Verdi's one-time mistress Teresa Stolz, a woman whose relationship with Verdi (as Meier documents) caused Giuseppina untold anguish. In his last years of decline, Stolz became Verdi's frequent visitor at Sant'Agata. In this, one of his very last letters, Verdi is 87 and she is 66:

We had some delightful hours, but they were too short. And who knows when even ones as short as those will come again! Oh an old man's life is truly unhappy! Even without real illness, life is a burden and I feel that vitality and strength are diminishing, each day more than the one before. I feel this within myself and I don't have the courage and power to keep busy with anything. Love me well and always, and believe in my love, which is great, very, very great, and very true.

Vitality, strength, courage, power: surely it is these qualities that Verdi gave to his music. At the very end of this letter there is also a tender expression of love and loyalty. Above all, we sense Verdi's uncompromising honesty and directness, his need to confront full in the face what the world offers, however unpalatable. This characteristic trait sometimes made him harsh and insensitive towards others, especially those who were close to him and who shared his life. But it also helped make his operas. We have to live with that contradiction: we probably shouldn't rejoice in it; however, we can – with the help of his music – understand that it is human.

But let's return to the works. I suggested earlier that we revive once-forgotten Verdi operas because his modern operatic equivalents simply do not exist. There's some truth in that, but it's not the whole truth. Think of an opera such as *Rigoletto*. My old teacher couldn't stand it; mainly, I think, because Verdi's dramatic world is so *direct*. People rush on, shout furious defiance at each other, wave swords, rush off again. They're propelled by an orchestra that is (at least until the final operas) unashamedly functional, often using simple rhythmic formulas to support the voices and inject energy. The drama comes thick and fast, and is over in the time a Wagner or a Berlioz would need for throat-clearing. This constant sense of pressure, which is there in the music as much as in the flow of events, used to be thought merely banal; but now, living as we do in a world where visual and sonic images flash before our eyes and ears in a bewildering and ever-accelerating stream, maybe we've found a fresh way to understand this directness. Perhaps we've even located within it a kind of emotional integrity that we now find increasingly hard to capture. Verdi's operas have somehow survived the coming and going of many fashions. They have proved themselves magnificently 'patient of interpretation', and will continue to pose questions that each generation will learn to answer in its own fashion. So long as opera survives, Verdi in some shape or form will continue to be with us.

ROGER PARKER

Early Setbacks · 1813–1840

The notes of the organ echoed round the little village church of San Michele and beyond as Giuseppe Verdi sat watching his teacher play. Don Baistrocchi was high up in the organ loft, above the heads of the congregation. The boy had waited all week long to hear this music, playing it over and over in his mind while he helped his mother serve in the tiny parlour of the inn, or assisted his father in the back room where they unpacked the provisions: salt, coffee, pickled meats, wine and spices.

In later years, when Verdi recalled his childhood, it was always *in poverty and darkness.*[1] He had been obliged to work for as long as he could remember, doing adult jobs from an early age, and he soon understood what it meant to be dependent on the generosity of others, on public assistance, and on benefactors. Throughout his life he remained sensitive to any form of dependent relationship.

The worst times for Verdi's family were in 1814, when the Austrian and Russian armies invaded, plundering and burning as they came, followed two years later by epidemics of typhus. Carlo Verdi and Luigia Uttini had been married in 1805. Both the Verdi and Uttini families were innkeepers from the province of Piacenza. Carlo Verdi ran a small inn – the Osteria Vecchia – at Le Roncole, a village in the Po plain north of Parma, from which he also sold provisions. He was often away from home fetching supplies, so his wife had to run the household, do the weaving, and see to the customers of the inn as well. When Giuseppe Fortunino Francesco

Verdi was born on 10 October 1813, his father was 30 and his mother 28. Two and a half years later a daughter was born, Giuseppa Francesca, but she died in 1833. Both children were named after their paternal grandparents, as was customary at the time, but since the Duchy of Parma belonged to France until 1815, Verdi's names were entered in the public register in their French form: Joseph Fortunin François.

His parents were firmly convinced that an education was vital for their son to get on in life, so they made every effort for him to gain one. This was not something to be taken for granted at a time when few children were able to go to school, particularly in country districts. The young Verdi (or Peppino as his family called him) was taught to read and write from the age of four by the village schoolmaster and organist, Pietro Baistrocchi, who also gave him his first lessons on the organ. Verdi was shy and serious as a child. Apparently he did not play games.[2] Music, however, held

San Michele Arcangelo in Le Roncole. In order to reach the organ loft Verdi had to climb up a ladder and through a trapdoor.

a great attraction for him, whether it was the melodies of itinerant fiddlers and hurdy-gurdy players or, more importantly, the music he heard in church. On one occasion he was so engrossed in listening to the organ that he forgot his duties as an acolyte and the priest kicked him, causing him to fall over. Verdi enjoyed telling the story of how he had cursed the priest, who had later been struck by lightning.

It was obvious from an early age what profession this musical child should follow – one day he would be the organist in Le Roncole. Carlo Verdi managed to buy a spinet (a small harpsichord) for his seven-year-old son and Verdi cherished this battered old instrument for the rest of his life. In the autumn of 1823 the ten-year-old Peppino was sent to secondary school in the neighbouring town of Busseto. His parents not only had to manage without his help at the inn, but they also had to find money for school books, food and lodging for their child. Verdi learned the value of money at an early age and it was a lesson he never forgot: in order *to be someone in the world* you had to climb up *from nothing* through hard work and determination.[3] Verdi and his old spinet moved in with a family in Busseto, where he received lessons in Italian and Latin, rhetoric and history at the school of Don Pietro Seletti.[4] Having learned the meaning of hard work, Peppino also found time to read books from the public library, to practise on his spinet in the evenings, and to walk the five kilometres to Le Roncole on Sundays and holy days in order to play for services in San Michele. He received 40 lire a year for playing the organ – mere pocket money. At the age of twelve he was appointed to the permanent job of organist. In the same year Verdi received his first professional lessons in harmony and composition at the music school run by the organist, conductor, composer, librettist, and schoolmaster in Busseto, Ferdinando Provesi. Verdi, who was Provesi's best pupil, started to teach himself the piano as well. But the pressures of school work, music school, and his position as organist soon began to tell on this shy and affable adolescent. When he was told off he would sometimes react in an unexpectedly violent and angry manner. Perhaps the fact that Verdi abandoned his music studies for a time shows how much he feared not being able to live up to the demands made on him or that he would be asked to leave school. It was only in 1827, after he had finished his studies (passing with distinction), that he could finally devote his entire time to music. Numerous compositions date from this period of study with Provesi: marches, trios, concertos and sacred works – but in old age, Verdi would destroy almost all of these early compositions. He was already giving lessons and playing in private concerts, and he received high praise for an overture to Rossini's *Il barbiere di Siviglia* (*The Barber of Seville*), with which he made his first public appearance.

One of the few child composers of true genius, Gioacchino Antonio Rossini (1792–1868) wrote 36 successful operas. The Viennese premiere of *Tancredi* in 1816 sent shock waves through the musical establishment, overturning the conventions of opera. Schubert described him as 'an extraordinary genius'. After writing *William Tell* (1829), ill-health forced him to almost stop composing. With the exception of the miraculous *Petite Messe Solenelle*, he wrote very little music, and famously devoted himself to gourmandising. In recent years, the prodigious works of his childhood have become widely admired, particularly his innovatory 6 Sonatas for 2 violins, cello and double-bass.

Other early Verdi pieces were also performed. Busseto, like many Italian towns, had a good amateur philharmonic society whose members formed both a choir with solo singers and an orchestra. If the large numbers of wind instruments, particularly clarinets and brass, meant that it sometimes sounded more like a military band, it nevertheless provided the young Verdi with a workshop where he could try out his new compositions and gauge their effect. The rehearsals and many of the concerts took place in the house of the society's president, Antonio Barezzi, which had a large salon.

In 1831, Barezzi – a wholesale grocer and merchant in his early forties who played several wind instruments – invited Verdi to live in his home. Here, Verdi became especially close to two of Barezzi's six children: the highly temperamental Margherita, who was almost exactly his age and a fellow pupil of Provesi, and her brother Giovanni, who remained a friend for a long time. Barezzi sponsored other music students, but his relationship with the young Verdi became almost that of father and son, developing an

There was a grand piano by Tomašek of Vienna in the salon of Barezzi's house, where Verdi rehearsed with the Philharmonic Society.

intimacy and trust that Verdi had never had with his own father. It would last for 38 years until Barezzi's death, and Verdi always remembered him as *so kind, so just, so sincere.*[5]

After he had finished his musical training in 1829, Verdi applied for the position of organist in nearby Soragna, but without success.

ANTONIO BAREZZI

He remained in Busseto for another three years, perhaps out of devotion to his new family, while continuing to play the organ in Le Roncole. He also substituted for his teacher, Provesi, who was often ill, at rehearsals and in concerts, and he composed for the Philharmonic Society. Barezzi was convinced that Verdi was *born for better things,*[6] and Provesi urged him to study at the Conservatory in Milan, the best and most modern in all Italy – but Verdi could not afford the fees. In 1830, Carlo Verdi had reluctantly left the Osteria Vecchia after getting behind with the rent and the family had moved to another house. The following year, Verdi's application for a scholarship from Monte di Pietà, a charitable foundation in the town, was unsuccessful, but his father had another plan. Carlo Verdi appealed to the charity of Duchess Maria Luigia of Parma, who granted his son a scholarship of 300 lire a year for four years. However, this was not finally approved until January 1832, so Barezzi stepped in to pay an advance for the first year. 'My son will never forget the magnanimity of his patron,' Carlo Verdi assured

The house belonging to Verdi's parents in Le Roncole. Carlo Verdi sold provisions at the rear of this Osteria

Barezzi in his letter of thanks, but it was then that things began to go wrong. Verdi failed the entrance examination to the Milan Conservatory, on which his own hopes and those of his friends and relatives plus the expectations of the philharmonic society had been so firmly set. It was obvious from his piano technique that he was self-taught and, at almost 19, he was well over the statutory age limit. To add insult to injury he was also treated like a foreigner in the kingdom of Lombardy-Venetia, which was part of Austria. Verdi never forgot this humiliation. Even at the age of 84 he was furious when it was proposed that the Milan Conservatory – which had *perpetrated* this *assault* on his *existence* half a century ago – should be named after him.[7]

One of the examiners advised Verdi to take private lessons with a colleague at the Conservatory, Vincenzo Lavigna, a former student of the opera composer Giovanni Paisiello (1740–1816), who had also for a time been harpsichordist and répétiteur at La Scala. Barezzi again magnanimously offered financial support. Later, in 1871, when Verdi advised music students to practise *diligently and consistently at fugues, until they were exhausted*, for only in this manner could they *learn to compose with confidence*,[8] he was also describing his own studies with Lavigna, who insisted on regular exercises in counterpoint. It is clear how much this early teaching influenced Verdi, since he returned again and again to the study of polyphonic music, and occasionally composed in polyphonic forms himself to the very end, with the fugue in *Falstaff*.

La Scala, Milan, the principal Italian opera house, opened in 1776. Noted for its varied repertoire, it attained its highest reputation under the direction of Arturo Toscanini (1867–1957).

Lavigna analysed countless scores with his student, introduced him to the Filodrammatici (a philharmonic society in Milan), and arranged for him to have a season ticket at La Scala. Verdi found lodgings in the old city with an acquaintance of Barezzi, the

The Teatro alla Scala in Milan.

teacher Giuseppe Seletti, but the relationship between Seletti and his 18-year-old lodger was difficult from the beginning. Verdi must have found it humiliating that Seletti not only decided on his pocket money but also on which items of clothing he could buy. Seletti treated him with scant kindness, with mistrust and criticism, and was displeased with Verdi's manners, his lack of polish, and his shabby clothes. He had to admit that the young man worked 'ceaselessly from morning to night' at his music, though he complained constantly in his letters to Barezzi about this 'disagreeable' lodger, whom he wished to be rid of as soon as possible.[9] Two years later, in the summer of 1834, Verdi took a room elsewhere.

Now he was near La Scala where the new operas of Vincenzo Bellini – *Norma* and *La Sonnambula* (*The Sleepwalking Girl*) – were playing, with performances that sent audiences into rapturous frenzies. Verdi was able to hear Giuditta Pasta (1797–1865) and Maria Malibran (1808–36), the celebrated prima donnas of bel canto, in operas by Bellini, Rossini, and Donizetti. Milan was an especially stimulating city with its medieval buildings, its baroque façades in the Austrian style, and its elegant streets. Masked balls were held at carnival time, and by the 1840s the city was newly illuminated by countless gas lamps. Fascinated by all these new impressions, Verdi tried to take at least some part in the elegant and extravagant life of the city, and no longer worked as hard as had been expected of him in the past. He soon found that a visit to the Teatro dei Filodrammatici, where the concerts of the philharmonic society were held, was just as interesting as Lavigna's tuition. When the harpsichordist fell ill during a rehearsal of Haydn's *Die Schöpfung* (*The Creation,* 1796–8), Verdi stepped in with both skill and enthusiasm to replace him – the accompaniment of the oratorio was immediately entrusted to this ambitious 20 year old. The director of the Filodrammatici, Pietro Massini, encouraged Verdi, but there was no permanent position available.

In 1833 the chance to escape from years of drudgery arrived from Busseto, where the position of *maestro di musica* (musical director), became vacant following the death of his old tutor Provesi. A bitter feud arose over the succession between a clerical faction and the town's Philharmonic Society, who exchanged public insults, circulated pamphlets, and even fought on the streets. Completely disregarding the proposal of an open competition, the bishop incurred the wrath of the Philharmonic Society by installing his own man as Maestro, the position for which Verdi had been preparing for so many years. Verdi travelled to Busseto in the summer

Vincenzo Bellini (1797–1835) died tragically young, only 6 weeks before his 34th birthday. However, in his short composing life, he wrote 11 operas, of which *La Sonnambula* and *Norma* are the most acclaimed. The expressive potency of his acrobatic vocal writing and mastery of *Bel Canto,*were very much the result of his careful study and analysis of the works of his forbears, Paisiello, Jommelli and Cimarosa.

After Cimarosa, Giovanni Paisiello (1740–1816) was the most succesful Italian opera composer of the late 18th Century, serving as the Kapellmeister to Catherine the Great in St Petersburg, and to Napoleon in Paris. He wrote over 90 operas and a beautiful piano concerto that had a great impact on Mozart. Paganini wrote variations, *Nel Cor Piu mi Sento,* on one of his arias.

MAESTRO DI MUSICA

of 1834, still hopeful that there would be a competition now that the Minister of the Interior had intervened. He even wrote to the Duchess of Parma for support. Avoiding the disputes between the various factions, Verdi worked hard with the Philharmonic Society, which had been without a conductor for a year. Symphonies and art song had scarcely any place in Italian musical life, so Verdi could only look for success as a composer of operas or sacred music (to which, as he confessed to Pietro Massini, he did not feel particularly drawn). He decided to compose an opera for the Teatro Filodrammatico, and went back to Milan at the beginning of the following year.

But in the summer of 1845, just when Verdi had finally found a suitable libretto – Lord Hamilton by Antonio Piazza – his supporters in Busseto pressed him to return. His benefactor Barezzi discreetly reminded him that he had already spent more than 1,400 lire that year on his behalf, and others put similar financial pressure on Verdi. The young composer felt as if he had *plunged into an abyss*. They could not *buy his humiliation and enslavement* with their charity, as he wrote to his teacher Lavigna, who had written him an excellent testimonial at the conclusion of his studies.[10] Nevertheless, Verdi did return to Busseto, mainly for the sake of Barezzi, and he remained there until February 1836 when the competition eventually took place. He won in convincing fashion, and in March he became the town's *maestro di musica*. Two months later he married Margherita Barezzi, his benefactor's daughter.

Although his father-in-law provided the newly-weds with a comfortable apartment, there were still financial worries. Verdi's salary was so meagre he quickly got into debt. These worries were added to by the birth of a daughter, Virginia, in March 1837, and of a son, Icilio Romano, in the summer of the following year. The children were named after the heroes of *Virginia*, the drama of liberation by Italy's leading pre-romantic poet and dramatist

Portrait of Margherita Barezzi by A Mussini. Verdi's first wife was the eldest daughter of Antonio Barezzi. She studied singing and was a trained music teacher.

Vittorio Alfieri (1749–1803) – and years before, at the age of 15, Verdi had composed a cantata, *I deliri di Saul*, based on one of Alfieri's best tragedies, *Saul*, with its romantic insistence on heroic willpower. Verdi had probably been supported in his political ideals by members of the Philharmonic Society in Milan, who were opposed to foreign rule by Austria and hoped for a united Italy, an independent 'Fatherland', as Alfieri called it. Since large parts of the country belonged to the Habsburgs or, following the Congress of Vienna, were under their rule, Austria was seen as the real opponent of unity and independence.

However hard Verdi worked in rehearsal and in concerts, as director of the music school and with a dozen or more private pupils, whom he taught a variety of subjects, and despite the support of Margherita, he could see no possibility of achieving great things in the provinces. He was composing all of the time – for instance, in 1838, six romances were printed, including settings from Goethe's *Faust* – and had made a name for himself in Busseto, but the fear remained that he was wasting his best years. He hoped his opera based on Lord Hamilton – probably *Rocester* (now lost) – would enable him to escape *from obscurity*.[11] By the autumn of 1836 he had completed it and was looking to get it performed,

but the Teatro dei Filodrammatic was no longer under Massini's direction, and in Parma, as in Milan, they shied away from the risk associated with producing an opera by a complete unknown. When Verdi finally begged Massini to intervene on his behalf with the powerful Bartolomeo Merelli – who had recently become the impresario at La Scala – it was like asking for a miracle.

In August 1838 their daughter Virginia died, and a month later Verdi and Margherita set off for Milan, as if hoping to force a change in their run of bad luck. At the beginning of the following year, with no firm contract, Verdi resigned from his secure position

Bartolomeo Merelli was one of the most influential theatre directors of his time. He was the director of La Scala during the period when five of Verdi's early operas were first performed there. After the failure of his *opera buffa*, Merelli wrote to reassure Verdi: 'I cannot force you to write, but my faith in you remains unshaken.'[12]

in Busseto and moved permanently with his family to the city. He felt like a swimmer who has *seen the bank he longs to reach* and is determined to *cling* to it.[13] Although Verdi and his wife were both teaching, they were more than ever dependent on Barezzi's support. Then, in the following spring, Merelli finally signed a contract to perform Verdi's opera – now revised and entitled *Oberto, Conte di San Bonifacio (Oberto, Count of Bonifacio)* – at La Scala.

There were many changes to be made to suit the singers who had just been engaged, and Merelli, formerly a librettist himself, made suggestions. He also sent Verdi to Temistocle Solera, who reworked Piazza's libretto. Nevertheless, the characters remained stiff and forced, and there were problems with the dramatic action. Oberto, defeated by his enemies, dishonoured and thirsting for revenge, seeks vengeance on the man who seduced his daughter. Oberto's sudden appearance at his wedding feast is reminiscent of the entry of the Commendatore in Mozart's *Don Giovanni* (1787). The finale of *Oberto*, a scene of terror, piles on the well-worn clichés as Oberto's daughter, the sacrificial Leonora, faces the cloister, madness, and death. With a libretto such as this Verdi had no hope of creating a new sort of opera to take the place of Rossini, Bellini, or Donizetti. Compared with Rossini, or with composers of his own generation

The Austrian composer Wolfgang Amadeus Mozart (1756–91) was born in Salzburg, the son of a violinist and composer. A precocious musical talent, he began his career at four and toured Europe at six. After a period of unhappy service with the Archbishop of Salzburg, he settled in Vienna in 1781, where he befriended Haydn and wrote his best music, including the operas *Le nozze di Figaro (The Marriage of Figaro*, 1786) and *Don Giovanni*. In his short life he composed 49 symphonies, more than 40 concertos, 6 string quintets, 26 string quartets, piano sonatas, violin sonatas, and much else besides. Some of his finest works include the operas *Così fan tutte, ossia la scuola degli amanti (Women are all the same, or The School for Lovers*, 1790), *Die Zauberflöte (The Magic Flute*, 1791), and the great symphonies: No 39 in E flat, No 40 in G minor, and No 41 in C (called the 'Jupiter'), all written in six weeks in 1788. His health was deteriorating while he composed his last work, the *Requiem Mass* in D minor, left unfinished at his death.

such as Berlioz, Mendelssohn, or Liszt, Verdi began his career in a conventional manner, writing cavatinas and arias to models that Bellini and Donizetti had already discarded. In *Oberto* the traditional

Joseph Haydn (1732–1809) was seen in the late 19th century as very much 'Papa Haydn', the *eminence grise* of Viennese late classicism. Despite his unquestioned importance, this perception owed much to the impact of Mozart and was further underlined by the notion that Beethoven was sent to Vienna to acquire 'the spirit of Mozart from the hands of Haydn'. Balakirev's view that he was 'that genius of petit-bourgeois music' died hard. It was not until the entire sweep of his innovatory symphonies, operas, chamber music and oratorios began to be appreciated in the 20th century that this somewhat myopic view gained clarity.

Remembering the composer Hector Berlioz (1803–1869), Verdi described him as 'as sick old man who railed at everyone', yet much of his work was indebted to the older man's both in it's huge dramatic ambition and instrumental richesse. Berlioz admired privately more than he chose to admit, for his reform of Italian music, and his integrity. He attended the premiere of *Don Carlos* in 1867. Berlioz' greatest orchestral work, his *Symphonie Fantastique* was inspired by his unrequited love for the English actress Harriet Smythson, whom he later married

with disastrous consequences. He was the first successful non-instrumentalist conductor.

German composer Felix Mendelssohn (1809–47) belongs with Chopin and Schumann to the early nineteenth-century classic-romantic school. A child prodigy, he made his public dêbut at nine and was a prolific composer at twelve, writing his overture to *A Midsummer Night's Dream* aged 17. In 1836 he became conductor of the Leipzig Gewandhaus orchestra and subsequently founded the Leipzig conservatoire. His works include five symphonies, overtures, the oratorios *St Paul* (1834–6) and *Elijah* (1846–7), chamber music, and music for piano.

Hungarian composer Ferencz (Franz) Liszt (1811–86) was also a virtuoso pianist. In 1848 he became Kapellmeister at the Weimar court and in the 1850s he wrote his *Faust Symphony* (1854–7) and *Dante Symphony* (1855–6). He invented a new art form with his symphonic poems – such as *Mazeppa* (1851), *Orpheus* (1853–4), and *Les Préludes* (1854) – and his harmonic innovations in works such as *Nuages gris* (1881) and *Csárdás macabre* (1881–2) anticipated the 'impressionism' of Debussy.

change of tempo from cantabile to cabaletta is often merely a matter of form, with no justification in the libretto.

Opera in nineteenth-century Italy appealed to a comparatively wide audience, replacing the theatre and popular drama, which were largely lacking, so opera had preserved an element of the folk tradition. This can be seen in marching rhythms; in music for brass (the 'banda'); in the choruses, which quickly achieved huge popularity; and above all in the distinction between melody and simple accompaniment. Hence the orchestra was often used like a guitar, accompanying the soloist in a regular chordal rhythm with an oompah-pah effect. However, Leonora's largo *Sciagurata!* in the finale of the second act shows that Verdi admired Bellini's *long, long, long melodies*[14] with irregular structures, in which no phrase is repeated and where the coloratura itself becomes the method of expression. The way in which Verdi created larger groups within the scenes, as in the trio in the first act and in the quartet of Act 2 of *Oberto*, indicates that he had already progressed beyond number opera. These ensembles, and the chorus in the finale of the first act with its four-part canon in a saraband rhythm expressing deep emotional shock, show that he was capable of leaving the conventional far behind.

Oberto had to be postponed to the following season, as one of the singers was ill, so the new cast again required changes. The fact that Verdi rewrote the baritone title role for the famous bass Ignazio Marini shows how much he was prepared to bow to the demands of the theatre. The première on 17 November 1839 was not exactly a triumph, but nevertheless *Oberto* did receive 14 performances that season. The major newspapers reviewed it, including the prestigious Paris *Revue et gazette musicale*. Merelli offered Verdi a contract for a further three operas and Giovanni Ricordi, proprietor of the largest music publisher in

The Italian Music publishing firm of Ricordi and Co, was founded in Milan in 1785 by the violinist and conductor Giovanni Ricordi, having studied music engraving at Breitkopf and Härtel, in Leipzing. He published the operas of Rossini, and later Verdi, and the firm went on to be the most distinguished and influential Italian publishing house. Giovanni's grandson, Guilio, discovered Puccini. The firm continues the tradition for publishing new music to this day, promoting the works, for instance, of Silvano Sciarrino and Franco Donatoni.

RICORDI AND CO.

Italy, bought the rights to the score for 2,000 lire.

But once again a shadow fell over Verdi's hard-won success. In October his young son Icilio had died. The illness and death of his children, financial worries, and his own exhaustion took their toll. A libretto by Gaetano Rossi, *Il Proscritto*, was lying on his desk, but inspiration failed. When Merelli, who needed an *opera buffa* for the following season, put renewed pressure on him, Verdi accepted the commission, albeit reluctantly. Of the various libretti offered him, *Un giorno di regno* by Bellini and Donizetti's librettist Felice Romani (1788–1865) seemed the only one even halfway acceptable. Despite its longueurs and confusions, it contained some comic situations and witty lines.

Then further tragedy struck. In June 1840 Margherita developed encephalitis and died. Devastated, Verdi broke off his work and travelled to Busseto where he hardly left his room in Barezzi's house. But the new opera buffa had already been announced for the autumn season and Merelli could not release him from his contract; so Verdi returned to his empty apartment in Milan. *Alone, alone,* grieving, ill, and under great pressure to meet his deadline, he devised music for Romani's comedy.[15]

Although he did not reach the heights of Rossini, whose operas he had probably studied with Lavigna, Verdi did follow his example. *Un giorno di regno* contains numerous deceptions and impersonations. Belfiore, in the guise of the Polish king Stanislas, sets in motion a series of misunderstandings which, by the end, have got so out of hand they can be resolved only through the deus ex machina of a letter from the genuine king. The duet between the baron and the treasurer, who cannot decide on the weapons to use in their duel, is a successful burlesque on macho rituals and poses. The simultaneous lyrical singing of the young lovers, with buffo chatter underneath in the sextet, is well realised, as is the Marchesa's floating cabaletta (*Se dee cader la vedova*). But it is all rather old-fashioned. Fashionable Milanese audiences no longer wanted to see *opera buffa*. They preferred the new *romanticismo* (romanticism) with its extremes of emotion and passion, like the heroines of Rossini's *Norma* and *La Sonnambula*, or Donizetti's *Lucia di Lammermoor* (1835). Added to this, the singers showed neither inclination nor talent for *opera buffa*, so the première of *Un giorno di regno* was a fiasco. Verdi, seated in the orchestra pit as was customary at the time, had to endure the hisses and catcalls of the audience. It was not an auspicious beginning to the young man's career.

Dreaming of Freedom · 1841–1849

In later years Verdi would occasionally exaggerate the importance of certain events in his past, but he was not wrong to say that a meeting with the impresario Merelli in 1840 changed his life for ever. Morelli had offered the German composer Otto Nicolai (1810–49) first refusal of a new libretto by Solera entitled *Nabucco*, but the German had turned it down, objecting that 'continual raging, blood-letting, cursing, physical violence, and murder were no suitable subject' for him.[16] So when Merelli met the griefstricken Verdi in the Galleria de Cristoforis he offered *Nabucco* to him, almost as an afterthought. Many years later Verdi takes up the tale:

Die Lustigen Weiben von Windsor, an opera 'after Shakespeare', was the most successful work of the German composer and conductor, Otto Nicolai (1810–1849). He died two months after its triumphant premiere at the Berlin Royal Opera, where he had been appointed Kapellmeister the year before. Nicolai was the founder of the Vienna Philharmonic Orchestra, and in 1887 his successor, Hans Richter, founded an annual 'Nicolai-Konzert' in his memory.

> *On the street I experienced an inexplicable feeling of sickness, of deep depression and distress that filled my heart. Returning home, I threw the manuscript down hard on the desk at which I stood. The libretto opened as it fell. For some unknown reason my eye was caught by the line on the page before me: 'Va pensiero, sull'ali dorate'.*[17]

'Fly thought on wings of gold' might be read as a metaphor for Verdi's own liberation, which suddenly seemed possible. Although his version of the opera's beginnings may not reflect the exact truth, it does suggest that the impression made on him by Solera's libretto was decisive. In this story about the subjection of a whole people, their imprisonment and eventual release, Verdi discovered a parallel to the experiences and dreams of his own people; and *Va pensiero, sull'ali dorate*, the opening line of the Chorus of the Hebrew Slaves (as it came to be known), provided the impetus for his opera *Nabucco*, which he finished in the autumn of 1841.

The captive Jews sing *Va pensiero* on the banks of the Euphrates. In its restrained and dreamlike opening, sung in unison, they remember their lost homeland. Then, at the beginning of the second stanza (*Arpa d'or*), the sudden fortissimo of the chorus, now in six parts and in a new key, seems to explode as if releasing some long pent-up emotion. Their inner feelings are described in broad sweeps of melody and varied rhythms, lingering in a long pianissimo final chord. The entire scene, entitled 'The Prophesy', shows how they grow in strength and confidence as they imagine their coming freedom, with its closing stretta, a warlike march with powerful syncopation, in the same rhythm as the slaves' chorus. This was the tune that Verdi's nationalist contemporaries would adopt to express the feelings of their people. It became a hymn for the awakening fatherland, a secular prayer.

The great choral scenes, like the one that opens the opera, are what give *Nabucco* its particular character and unity. The voices of both the men and the women in varying combinations and different words express the feelings they hold in common: panic and deadly fear, grief and longing for their homeland, hope, readiness to fight and joy. The chorus of the Levites in Act 2 (*Il maledetto non ha fratelli*) demonstrates how they show no mercy in expelling the traitors. It is an early example of Verdi's staccato choruses, sung *sotto voce*, in which the music takes on a life of its own with sharply pointed syncopation in the climaxes. The chorus goes way beyond its traditional function of simply opening and closing each act and underpinning an ensemble, to become one of the *dramatis personae* in its own right: the force of the people's suffering.

Nabucco and Abigaille, the two outstanding protagonists, represent those who exercise power, which has both formed and corrupted them. Nabucco, King of Babylon, is used to victory. He does not conceal the enjoyment with which he wields power, as can be seen from his *presto*, sung with *wild joy*, which introduces the final ensemble of the first act. In the final quartet of the second act, when he sings of the terror that paralyses all those in his presence, it demonstrates his cynical delight in the helplessness of others. It is only when his downfall is predicted in the finale of the second act that he is seen to be human; he is in pain, perhaps even mad (*Oh! mia figlia!*).

Abigaille's demands and fantasies of power stem from a slave's longing for identity, which leads to disintegration and excess; as portrayed in the nervous rhythms and broad melodic intervals.

-lei,   che il so - lo   mio ben con - ten - de,   sa

Very high virtuoso coloratura, huge leaps and fast runs show coldness, aggression and power. The final scene reveals the extremes to which the character of Abigaille is subjected – her plea for forgiveness as she dies is given particular expressiveness by an ostinato cello motif and the lament of the cor anglais. An example of the vividness and the exaggeration with which Verdi still sometimes portrayed his characters can be found in the scene between Nabucco and Abigaille in Act 3: a boisterous, almost cheeky woodwind tune illustrates Abigaille's anticipation of victory while the King begs for mercy.

Occasional exaggeration of this sort and Verdi's free use of theatrical effects show that *Nabucco* was not written with just an educated audience in mind. The use of repeated motifs, instrumental colouring, and sequences that are easy to recognise and follow, were all designed to make this opera generally accessible. Verdi's musical shorthand includes such conventional codes as the diminished seventh indicating terror (the cry *Abigaille!* in Act 1, for example); chromatic scales for pain; dotted marcato rhythms in military situations; declamation on a single note to express menace; reintroduction of earlier motifs for moments of recollection (as in Nabucco's dream); and flute arpeggios to represent sounds from another world (which accompany Nabucco's prayer and Abigaille as she dies). Despite the many parallels with Rossini's *Mosè in Egitto* (*Moses in Egypt*, 1818), there is clear evidence in *Nabucco* that Verdi liberated himself from the models of his predecessors in musical construction. Individual numbers no longer merely follow one another. Here the four acts instead build to huge, self-contained tableaux. Of course the audience already knew the patriotic choruses and warlike march rhythms from operas by Rossini – and Bellini's wild military chorus 'Guerra, guerra' from *Norma*, with its hatred of the Roman invaders, was sung everywhere – but choral scenes on such a grand scale as those of *Nabucco* were hailed as something quite new. The forceful way in which Verdi pressed Merelli to produce the work in the forthcoming carnival season – although La Scala had three new operas already planned – shows how important *Nabucco* was for the composer.

The soprano Giuseppina Strepponi, in the virtuoso role of Abigaille, could not match the famous baritone Giorgio Ronconi as Nabucco. Born in Lodi, south-east of Milan, in 1815, Giuseppina was only 26, but she was already long past the peak of her career. She had met Verdi three years before when she had given her support to the first performance of *Oberto*. Immediately after she had finished her studies at the Milan Conservatory she had accepted engagement after engagement in order to support her mother, brothers, and sisters. She had a beautiful high soprano voice, was intelligent, pretty, and a good actress, so success came early. Despite vocal strain, health problems, and several pregnancies, she seemed to be constantly on stage, and began to suffer from coughing fits that soon ruined her voice, as the critics were not slow to point out. To Verdi's surprise, Giuseppina Strepponi managed eight performances in *Nabucco*, although plagued by breathing problems, but the role had to be recast for the 57 performances in the following season. The opera was performed more than 100 times at La Scala alone in the eight years to 1850.

The première of *Nabucco* on 9 March 1842 made Verdi a star. This shy young composer from the provinces, who still shared an apartment with Giovanni Barezzi and who had the support of a mere handful of musicians in Milan, suddenly found himself

Giuseppina Strepponi was Verdi's champion from the very beginning. She sang the soprano roles in *Nabucco* and *Ernani*, but had to abandon her career at 30 as her voice was ruined

exposed to the glare of publicity. People wanted his portrait or clamoured for hats and scarves à la Verdi. Barrel organs played his tunes and he was a fashionable topic of conversation in aristocratic salons. He was invited to the soirées of the Countesses Maffei, Somaglia, Appiani, and Morosini, where intellectuals, scientists, artists, and journalists met, many of them opponents of Austrian rule. People talked about further French reforms, about the possibility of a constitutional state, and without doubt also about the 'Young Italy' movement, the patriotic revolutionary Giuseppe Mazzini's secret society. Countess Clara Maffei was a fervent patriot, in contrast to her more conservative husband. In her salon Verdi met aristocrats and middle-class intellectuals – men such as Arrivabene, Carcano, Grossi, Manara, Tenca, and Toccagni – who were fighting for a united, independent Italy.

Verdi was fascinated by these discussions on politics and art, by the elegant lifestyle, and by these wealthy hostesses who so despised convention, in particular Donna Emilia Morosini, to whom he wrote some rather effusive letters. Later he became an admirer of the Countess Appiani, but however much he tried to pose as a charming and gallant man-about-town, Verdi remained an outsider. He could not always conceal his impatience, his nervousness, or his irritability, and what with so many deadlines

Italian patriot and revolutionary Giuseppe Mazzini (1805–72) had an intensely religious belief in the spiritual progress of mankind towards unity and brotherhood. Nevertheless, he condoned the use of violence in the pursuit of Italian independence. Disillusioned by the failed uprising in 1831, he formed a clandestine society, Giovane Italia and demanded an independent, united republic of Italy. Banished from Switzerland in 1836, he lived for much of the remainder of his life in London, although he was called to office in the short-lived Roman republic of 1848. National unity was achieved in 1860, but although Mazzini was now a hero of the nationalist movement he was forced to remain in exile. In 1868 he moved to Switzerland, and in 1872 he returned in disguise to Italy to die. There were 80,000 mourners at his funeral in Genoa.

YOUNG ITALY

Clara Maffei's famous salon became the meeting place for artists, intellectuals, and patriots for a quarter of a century.

Emilia Morosini was another member of the patriotic aristocracy who held a regular salon in Milan and who gave Verdi her full support.

to meet he was frequently ill with stomach trouble, bronchitis, or attacks of rheumatism.

In 1842 he began to invest his earnings in property. Two years later he bought the holding Il Pulgaro in Le Roncole, with 25 hectares of meadow and vineyards, where his parents then went to live. By 1845 he was able to acquire one of the handsomest houses in Busseto, the Palazzo Cavalli – today the Palazzo Orlandi – very close to Barezzi's house. Big cities and famous Italian landscapes held no attraction for him. He preferred familiar surroundings: the misty, arid plain, the severity of secluded avenues lined with poplars, and above a wide expanse of sky.

An opportunity to display his new-found creative power was provided by his next commission from Merelli, who left it to the composer to fix the level of his fee. On the advice of Giuseppina Strepponi, Verdi demanded 9,000 Austrian lire – 1,000 lire more than Bellini had received for *Norma* and more than 13 times the annual salary Verdi had received as Busseto's *maestro di musica*. However, public expectation that he would repeat the success of *Nabucco* hindered the progress of his next opera, *I Lombardi alla prima crociata (The Lombards at the First Crusade)*, for which Solera was again writing the libretto.

Although the subject is another confrontation between cultures and religions, in contrast to *Nabucco* the connection between national destiny and personal conflict remains casual. Perhaps too keen to repeat his popular success, Verdi incorporated certain special effects into his music: a Turkish background; battle music; an obligato violin in the style of Paganini; a heavenly vision; and above all, striking contrasts. Vast stretches of the music are marked *con slancio* ('with impetuosity'), and the spirited crusader theme, the military songs and marches obscure the reality of war, to which Giselda's plea against *godless mass murder* stands in contrast. The stage set (which at one point featured Milan's Sant'Ambrogio Church), the title, and many of the musical numbers would no doubt have aroused patriotic sentiments in the Milan audiences.

The greatest of all violinists, Niccolo Paganini (1782–1840) stood on the mosts potent fault line of Romanticism; as a classicising force, embodied in the phenomenal technical clarity of his playing, reflected in Ingres' spectacular silverpoint drawing of him, or as the demonic figure of the possessed virtuoso, as Delacroix put it: 'There is the inventor! There is the man who is truly fitted for his art!' Hector Berlioz was inspired by both his mien and his playing, to compose the symphonic poem, 'Harold in Italy' for him, where he, the soloist, playing the viola, was to be the embodiment of Byron's wandering romantic hero, 'Childe Harolde'. Paganini refused to play it. From 1834, crippled both by debts, after his 'Casino Paganini' failed, and cancer of the larynx, he disappeared from public view. His *Del Gesu* violin *il canone*, as he called it, is on show in his home town of Genoa.

Since the spring of 1844 Verdi had been sharing his solitary working life with Emanuele Muzio. They had been friends from the time when Muzio, the son of a cobbler from a village near Busseto, had

EMANUELE MUZIO

been a pupil of Verdi's wife. When Muzio, with Barezzi's support, received a scholarship from the Monte di Pietà, he became Verdi's pupil. Verdi, twelve years Muzio's senior, helped him to rise *from nothing*, as he himself had done,[18] and he cared for the 19-year-old almost like a father. Muzio always referred to Verdi as 'Signor Maestro' in his many enthusiastic letters to Barezzi. Every morning Verdi gave him lessons in counterpoint and composition. He also taught him good manners and took care of his wardrobe and finances. Muzio acted as secretary for his teacher; he copied vocal parts, prepared piano reductions, and in addition made breakfast and nursed Verdi when he was ill. They worked at the same table, ate together at midday, and occasionally played cards or billiards. Muzio's admiration for his teacher was unconditional, and he remained his devoted colleague for 50 years.

'Signor Maestro Verdi has been giving me lessons in counterpoint . . . Many music students would have to pay two or even three talers for a lesson, if the Maestro would agree to teach them. But he does not give lessons to anyone except for this one poor devil, on whom he has bestowed a thousand benefits . . . He is so magnanimous, so noble-minded, and so clever, and he has such a large heart that, were one to search for his equal, one could think only of yourself.'
The 19-year-old Emanuele Muzio to Antonio Barezzi in 1844.[19]

In the eight years from the success of *Nabucco* to 1850, Verdi wrote twelve further operas and revised *I Lombardi*. He was composing almost without interruption, so that he could produce each year at least one première, sometimes as many as three. His rivals were few and far between. Giovanni Pacini (1796–1867) and Saverio Mercadante (1795–1870) were no longer serious competition; Bellini had died in 1835; Rossini – whom Verdi visited in Bologna in the summer of 1842 – had long since ceased to compose; and Donizetti was so ill that he wrote little after 1844. The way was clear for Verdi to become the most important opera composer in Italy.

The dramatic impetus in Verdi's early operas came from the sequence of numbers. These had to be as varied as possible and

were to some extent interchangeable since his librettists constantly
invented new situations in which
to express familiar sentiments:
love and hate, patriotism, anger,
wounded honour, indecision, and
grief. Dream narratives may

The works of Saverio Mercadante
(1795–1870) include 60 operas and 6
flute concerti. Rossini commissioned
him to write *I Briganti*. Later in life his
output slowed, partially due to his
bitter feud with Verdi. He went blind
in 1862, but dictated his final work,
Il lamento del bardo that year.

be worked into this sequence – as in *Alzira* (1845); *Giovanna d'Arco*
(*Joan of Arc*, 1844–5); *Attila* (1845–6); and *I masnadieri* (*The Robbers*,
1846–7) – and there is nearly always a *preghiera* (prayer), often with
harp accompaniment. Elements of the contemporary fashion for
Gothic horror put in an appearance: choirs of angels and demons
in *Giovanna d'Arco*; the prison scenes in *I due Foscari* (*The Two Foscari*,
1844) and *Il corsaro* (*The Corsair*, 1847–8); nocturnal scenes throughout *Attila*; eerie settings like the crypt in *Ernani* (1843–4); and the
subterranean vault in which the Knights of Death take their oath
in *La battaglia di Legnano* (*The Battle of Legnano*, 1848–9). In these
early works Verdi's protagonists are still not outstanding individuals whose characters develop in any meaningful sense. The
cast list remains constant: the lovers (soprano and tenor) and their
opponent (baritone). However, he did create powerful father figures
before *Rigoletto* (1850–1): Oberto, Nabucco, Francesco Foscari,
Count Moor, and the elderly Miller – fathers who suffer because
of their children, powerless despite their stubborn inflexibility,
representatives of an increasingly fragile patriarchal society. There
is always a death scene to end the opera, which often includes a
vision of heaven in which a utopian reconciliation takes place.
Most of the numbers are in standard form: introduction; two
movement arias or duets, with or without chorus – all finishing
with the obligatory cabaletta (which almost always interrupts
the dramatic action since it more or less demands applause); then
a finale in which a concentration of sound and an acceleration

of tempo into the stretta are used for effect. The function of the orchestra is often restricted to a chordal accompaniment for the singers, supporting them in expressive phrases *colla voce*, with the exception of a few notable illustrative passages. Verdi was, however, refining his technique, and from *Nabucco* onwards always sketched out his ideas before writing a final version. In place of the potpourri type of overture, we often find individual preludes that refer directly to the protagonist. Tone colouring also becomes more subtle. Whereas in early ensembles the same melody might be used to portray a variety of sentiments, in later ensembles Verdi was able to express different feelings simultaneously.

These operas were written to commission with fixed deadlines, so Verdi was constantly working under pressure. The financial risk was borne by the impresario alone. He engaged the singers at his own expense, planned the forthcoming season and commissioned new operas. The impresario was therefore understandably anxious that deadlines be met, and occasionally these demands were legally enforced. When Verdi was unable to deliver his opera *Alzira* on time because of illness, he managed to escape a fine only by producing a doctor's certificate. In his contracts for *Attila*, *I masnadieri*, and *Il corsaro* with his publisher Francesco Lucca, Verdi also sold the performance rights, so Lucca was ultimately responsible for all the conditions of performance. Eventually relations with this publisher, an extremely hard bargainer – *inconsiderate, impertinent, and insatiable*, in Verdi's opinion[20] – were severed. The speed with which he had to complete his operas left little time for reflection, for study, or for experimentation. He wrote later of his *sixteen years' hard labour* following *Nabucco*,[21] and of a workload for which he needed the *head and shoulders of a furniture remover*; he was weary of theatre business and of constantly churning out scores. Maybe he was also feeling dissatisfied with the shortcomings of these production-line operas. *My soul looks black*, he wrote to a friend in the winter of 1845, *perpetually black, and it will remain thus until I have left this career, which I loathe, behind me.*[22]

Verdi's audiences were not complaining. Most of his works were received with enthusiasm. *Ernani* and *Attila* played successfully in several cities, and the composer was offered many a laurel wreath

Caricature of Verdi by Melchiorre Delfico: *Thank you for your news about* Alzira, *and even more for remembering your poor friend who is condemned to scribble away at his music. God protect the ears of any good Christian who has to listen to it! Cursed music!*[23]

and adulatory verse; but he was constantly dissatisfied. *I still have to write six operas, then I shall bid farewell to all this,* he wrote in 1845.[24] He had always wanted *to be someone,*[25] but it was because he had never forgotten the shock of sudden disaster that he allowed himself to be harnessed to the yoke of the opera business. Despite the applause of many, despite the high regard and the demonstrable sympathy with which he was received, his dissatisfaction continued to grow, although he struggled to master it. He noticed how often he was out of temper and irritated, and from time to time he mocked himself for all his *eccentricities, moods,* and *ill humours,* which, he freely admitted, were *sometimes unbearable*.[26] When he repeatedly said of himself that he was at bottom a *farmer*[27] there was of course an element of exaggeration, but he also doubted his artistic achievement. Reviewers commented on his failings, of course. They criticised his 'noisy' music,[28] the marches, the stereotyped cabalettas and strettas, the lack of variety in the orchestration, which was often put together at the last minute. Conservative critics also accused him of corrupting the noble art of coloratura with his declamatory style. Compared to the artificial vocal embellishments of bel canto, Verdi's simple syllabic tunes seemed almost vulgar. Verdi appeared to accept the fate of his operas with equanimity: the failure of *I Lombardi* in Venice in 1843; the cool reception of *Giovanna d'Arco* at the Milan première in 1845; the merely polite applause for *I due Foscari* at La Scala; the disappointment after the extravagant Paris première of *Jérusalem* (the French version of *I Lombardi*, 1847); and the fiasco of *Il corsaro*. The critics had remarked on the banality of the music in *Alzira*, and a ditty about Verdi's gradual decline was making the rounds in Naples. The verdict of the critics affected him, of course, although he was sceptical about success or failure. He always remained mistrustful of the public, although he accepted that *for three lire the audience buys the right to hiss or applaud*.[29]

A lithograph of Verdi by Richter after a drawing by L De Crescenzo. The composer, who was at that time 32, looked considerably older. 'Signs of anxieties and illness, as well as deep reflection, are to be seen in his face.' *Illustrated London News*.[30]

It was taking Verdi longer and longer to find suitable operatic material. To a large extent the subject he chose depended on which singers were engaged by the theatre where the opera was to be staged: was a good tenor available for the main role, perhaps Antonio Poggi or Gaetano Fraschini? Or perhaps a baritone instead, such as Giorgio Ronconi or Felice Varesi? As a rule, Verdi took the vocal range of the singer into consideration when he was composing, and he sometimes wrote special cabalettas with particular singers in mind, since to a large extent the success of an opera depended on them.

Verdi did not wish to repeat

Poet, dramatist, and novelist Victor (Marie) Hugo (1802–85) was the most prolific and versatile of the French Romantics. In 1827 his *Préface de 'Cromwell'* (see page 36) established him as the leader of the Romantic movement. He is best known for his novels *Notre-Dame de Paris* (*The Hunchback of Notre-Dame*, 1831) and *Les Misérables* (1862), his plays *Hernani* (1831) and *Ruy Blas* (1838), and his poems in *Les Contemplations* (1856). In the 1840s he became involved in republican politics, and after the coup by the future Napoleon III he went into exile in Jersey until 1855, then in Guernsey until 1870. A national hero on his return to France, he was buried in the Panthéon.

himself after *Nabucco* and *I Lombardi*, so he looked for new subjects in Romantic literature. For *Ernani* he set a libretto based on a play by the Victor Hugo, while *I due Foscari* and *Il corsaro* drew inspira-

tion from works by Lord Byron. However, the censors – who in Milan were under the control of the Cardinal Archbishop Gaetano Gaisruck and the chief of police Luigi Torresani – had raised objections to *I Lombardi*, so it was inevitable that such notorious writers as Hugo and Byron would attract their attention. This clash of religious, moral, and political views in the censorship of theatrical productions led to some comic

English poet George Gordon, Lord Byron (1788–1824) found fame with the publication of *Childe Harolde's Pilgrimage* (1812). After a failed marriage he left England in 1816 to stay near Geneva with the poet Percy Bysshe Shelley (1792–1822). He then lived a riotous life in Venice where he completed *Manfred* (1817) and began the satire *Don Juan* (1819). His poems *The Corsair* (1814) and *The Two Foscari* (1821) inspired two operas by Verdi. He died in Greece while training troops at Missolonghi, involved in the Greek struggle for independence from Turkey.

situations. For instance, in Milan the amount of applause permitted in the opera house was regulated, as was the number of curtain calls. In Venice the title *I due Foscari* was forbidden because families with this surname were living there; so the première took place in Rome instead. The 'Ave Maria' in *I Lombardi* was regarded as sacrilegious, so became 'Salve Maria'. Neither robbers nor members of the nobility could be portrayed as operatic heroes in some opera houses, and most definitely not aristocrats turned bandits, as in *Ernani*. In order to keep the patriotic fervour of the audience within bounds, after the première of *La battaglia di Legnano* (which had occurred in 'liberated' Rome) the battle scene had to be transferred to Holland for subsequent performances, so that Barbarossa became the Duke of Alba, and the opera was now entitled *L'assedio di Arlem (The Uprising in Harlem)*. There was every reason for the government to fear attacks on the authority of the State, even in the opera houses. The audience was delighted to detect any allusion to the suppression of Italy. Under Metternich's system of surveillance, theatres were closed, passports were withdrawn, and fortunes confiscated. Composers were even threatened with imprisonment or death.

Austrian statesman Prince Klemens von Metternich (1773–1859) took the most prominent role at the Congress of Vienna. He was the leading figure in European diplomacy after the defeat and exile of Napoleon. He had been the minister for Austrian foreign affairs since 1809, some years before the fall of the French Emperor to whose demise he relentlessly devoted himself. Metternich acted as the restorer of the 'old regimes', reinstating the old monarchies. He supressed all popular aspirations to liberalism within the Austrian Empire. After the collapse of the imperial government in the 1848 revolutions, he fled to England.

Verdi had known poverty and debt at an early age, and subsequently the uncertain life of a theatre composer, so he paid special attention to the details of his contracts with individual opera houses – La Scala; later La Fenice in Venice (the most important opera house in Italy after La Scala); the Teatro Argentina in Rome;

the San Carlo in Naples; and the Teatro della Pergola in Florence. He set out exactly the level of his fee and the dates when payments were due, the rights to the score, and most importantly, he insisted on himself selecting the singers from the company in question. He proved to be a hard negotiator right from the start, and was unwilling to depart from the conditions of his contract *for anything in the world.*[31] He would not accept that the final payment of his fee should be due after the third performance, *since for a thousand reasons the third performance might not take place;*[32] the sum was therefore to be paid after the first performance.

He devoted enormous time and effort to his work, often putting in more than ten hours a day; working with librettists, the impresario, the publisher, and the censors; corresponding with agents, journalists, and singers, whose tantrums caused him additional work; and he demanded an equal commitment from the singers, who sometimes cursed him when they had to endure numerous rehearsals and complained of his abrupt manner.

Verdi frequently suffered from chronic throat infections and stomach pains. The Venetian winter climate did not suit him; he had rheumatic attacks, and his bronchitis gave rise to his greatest fear: tuberculosis. He found some relief in the autumn of 1845 at Clara Maffei's country villa in Cluson, but over Christmas he again suffered a severe bronchial attack. He recovered his health only in the high air of Recoaro, where he spent the summer.

Although Verdi's meetings with the soprano Giuseppina Strepponi during this period were never extended, they saw each other frequently. She continued to advise him and to write letters on his behalf. She was rumoured to have had countless affairs. She had a son, Camillo,[33] fathered by Cirelli, one of her agents, and a daughter, Giuseppa Faustina, the following year. Both children grew up in an orphanage, while a daughter born in 1841 died in infancy. After an extended period of illness, only the smaller theatres were prepared to offer her parts and, eventually, when no one would engage her at all, she was obliged to advertise for a position. She finally decided in the autumn of 1846 to open a school for singers in Paris. In October of that year she received a letter from Verdi, which she sealed after she had read it and which she kept until her death as her most treasured possession. She wrote on the envelope: 'This letter is to be placed on my heart when I am buried!' To this day it lies unopened in the archives of Sant'Agata (for it was discovered only after her funeral).

Verdi's first work for La Fenice was to be an opera based on Victor Hugo's play *Hernani* (1830). The librettist was Francesco Maria Piave, a proof-reader, translator, and editor in Venice. Three years younger than Verdi, he had little experience of writing libretti. After he had read a few scenes of *Ernani*, Verdi asked Piave in astonishment: *Where can we find a prima donna who can sing in succession a long cavatina, a duet ending in a trio and then a whole finale? . . . Where is the maestro who can set to music 100 verses of recitative without becoming boring?*[34] Verdi worked more intensively on the text than usual. This close collaboration meant he was a major influence on the libretto, sketching out scenarios himself and then demanding that Piave provide *a particularly detailed synopsis,* so that he could put in his own ideas.[35] His many letters to the librettist reveal a close friendship, warm and gruff, although Piave also had to put up with some harsh criticism and even downright rudeness. He proved to be amenable, patient, and ever willing to adapt, and tried to follow Verdi's instructions as best he could. He was sometimes rather casual, so the impatient Verdi was continually urging speed – *Pull yourself together, no sleeping, hurry up!*[36] – and then making fun of unsuccessful passages: *You're always so long-winded!*[37] Verdi was genuinely fond of Piave – or the *tomcat,* as he called him occasionally – although he treated him like a dim-witted schoolboy from time to time, and delivered a hurtful snub when he disliked his libretto for *Macbeth*, sending it straight to the writer and translator Andrea Maffei (the husband of Countess Clara Maffei), for further work. In the end Piave's name did not appear at all on the published text.

Although Shakespeare's plays were rarely performed in Italy, Verdi greatly admired their realism; and he had the opportunity to discuss Shakespeare with Giulio Carcano, who had translated the complete works into Italian, at Countess Maffei's soirées. Verdi was fascinated above all by *Macbeth* (*c*.1606), and decided to make it

Francesco Maria Piave – known to his friends because of his wild hair and his hoarse voice as the 'Goth' or the 'Teuton' – wrote nine libretti for Verdi, who was always complaining to him: *Remember to use few words . . . few words . . . few, but with character!'*

the subject of his next opera for Florence. *This tragedy is one of the greatest works of human endeavour!* he wrote to Piave, who was to set Verdi's scene sketches into verse. *Bear always in mind that there must be no superfluous word in the text: Everything must be significant . . . And, I beseech you, do not be unkind to this Macbet* [sic]; *I beg you on my knees.*[38] It was daring to write an opera in Italy without a pair of lovers and with no leading role for a tenor, but the greatest loss was felt in the massive textual cuts, which had been unproblematic in an opera such as *Ernani*. The resulting libretto was now inadequate to fully justify the actions of the characters, and so emotions took centre stage. Whereas Verdi had sometimes bothered little

Shakespeare's plays first became known in Italian translation in the mid 18th century. German versions appeared from the 1780's. Beethoven, Mendelssohn, Berlioz and Liszt all found inspiration in Shakespeare's work, and since that time, it can safely be said that no secular writer has had a greater impact on the language and aesthetics of music.

about the texts of his earlier operas, here he found fault with much in Piave's writing. He corrected, he elucidated, he poked fun, and he urged speed. He had been able to secure the excellent baritone, Felice Varesi, for the role of Macbeth, and corresponded with him about questions of characterisation, about the reading of particular lines, and the meaning of certain expression marks. On the other hand, Verdi rejected Eugenia Tadolini, originally cast to sing the role of Lady Macbeth, because she had a *wonderful, clear, pure, and powerful voice*, whereas Lady Macbeth should be *ugly and evil*, and have a *rough, choked, sombre* voice.[39] Verdi was here following the aesthetic principle of Victor Hugo, as formulated in his Romantic manifesto the *Preface to 'Cromwell'* (1827). The important thing was to portray 'not beauty but character'. Since the subject of drama was life itself, in which the grotesque must be allowed to take its place alongside the sublime, this was the 'greatest beauty of drama'. Hugo's view that 'the vulgar and the trivial' had their proper place in drama was the justification for Verdi's presentation of the witches' choruses, which were to be *vulgar, fantastic, and original*.[40]

During rehearsals he became more demanding than ever. Shortly before the public dress rehearsal, as the audience was arriving in the auditorium, and when the orchestra was already seated, he insisted on yet another piano rehearsal of the duet between the two protagonists. Marianna Barbieri-Nini, now singing Lady Macbeth, reported Varesi's objection that they had already rehearsed this 150 times. Then this would be the 151st, retorted Verdi, although the audience was becoming restless.

The première in the Teatro della Pergola on 14 March 1847 was received with much applause, but the critical notices were more reserved. While critics admired the instrumental writing, they found that *Macbeth* lagged considerably behind Weber's *Der Freischütz* (*The Freeshooter*, 1817–21) or Meyerbeer's *Robert le diable* (1831).

Verdi, however, set such store by this new opera that he refused to allow Ricordi to perform *Macbeth* at La Scala. Two years previously he had had problems with Merelli, who was in financial difficulties and was making as many savings as possible on the chorus, orchestra, sets, costumes, and rehearsals, so that he could still afford to hire expensive virtuoso singers. A disparaging remark by Merelli about *Attila* led to a final break in their friendship. Disgusted with *the miserable way* in which his operas were staged at La Scala, Verdi decided that in future he would allow none of them to be performed there. He dedicated *Macbeth* to Antonio Barezzi, his *father, benefactor, and friend* as a token of his *eternal remembrance, gratitude, and love.*[41]

The composer, pianist and conductor Carl Maria Weber (1786–1826) established a truly autonomous school of German Romantic opera, as well as evangelising Beethoven's large choral and symphonic works. His reputation rests on three operatic works, especially *Der Freischütz,* but he was equally innovative in other areas, particularly in providing virtuoso works for the clarinet and viola of unprecedented expressiveness.

Eighteen years later Verdi carefully revised this darkest of his operas, which goes to show how highly he valued it. Two of the original scenes, a duet and the sleepwalking scene, clearly demonstrate his new and highly experimental method of composition, and they remain unchanged in the Paris version of 1865. In the duet between Macbeth and Lady Macbeth in the first act, the first part, the recitative, is particularly impressive for its orchestral colour and instrumental motifs, and for the dissonance of its harmonies and its contrasting tempi, as Macbeth portrays his horror of the crime (the offstage murder of the King), finally singing *Tutto è finito!* ('It is done!') *with choking voice* in a tense silence. Dark minor keys, cor anglais, low clarinets, and muted strings colour the entire scene. The limited number of orchestral motifs confer unity, while the use of chromatic scales, the minor second and particularly an oscillating motif in many variations and different tempi, mirror the nervous anxiety of the protagonists and their utter inability to act. The music gradually breaks down when the melody of the first cantabile in F minor grinds to a halt, degenerating into speech-like declamation and ending in plaintive cries. In marked contrast to the severity with which Macbeth judges himself is the sinuous legato motif sung by Lady Macbeth, whose efforts to tempt her husband and spur him to greater heights cannot hide the fear and horror to be heard in the music. Lady Macbeth, as temptress, exemplifies the link between eroticism and force when she later sings of the 'pleasure' she felt in exercising power, and enlivens those present with a drinking song. As she tries to soothe Macbeth with her scherzando motif, their two parts do not reveal unanimity, but rather a brutal lack of understanding. Against all expectations in an opera duet, the three 'arioso' sections end quietly, *morendo,* including the final short presto, by the end of which Macbeth's voice is reduced to a stammer.

In contrast to the chorus of demons in *Giovanna d'Arco,* the witches (Verdi stipulated 18 singers) are not an allegory of evil. They have many faces and speak in many voices: light and brilliant (*Le sorelle vagabonde*); unctuous (*Salve, o Macbetto*); or as conspirators (*Fuggiam, fuggiam*). Their choruses and dances do not differ essentially from the music Verdi wrote for large groups in his other operas, but here the tone is harsher, the vulgar more prominent – for instance the menacing brass tune with the stamping of the basses, or the wild waltz of the ballet music in the third act. The facelessness of the witches and their indifference to the fate of the individual again indicate the increasing anonymity of society. If what is to happen has already been prophesied, the individual feels no responsibility to assert himself. After meeting the witches Macbeth's voice is stifled (in Verdi's directions) as if all ability to make decisions had already been taken from him.

It is no 'gentle' madness like Norma's that introduces the *great sleep-walking scene* in the last act, but a terrible deformation and final annihilation of self. Lady Macbeth's monologue is no longer composed as an aria. There are neither verses nor repeated sections. Often we hear only fragments of melody with a semitone motif, and instead of being accompanied by chorus and ensemble (which usually enhance great arias) there is only the almost whispered, uncomprehending commentary of two onlookers. The unity of the scene is created by the bleak instrumental colour (low clarinets, cor anglais, muted strings and timpani) and by the orchestral motifs: a repeated ghostly tapping, an agonising suspension obsessively repeated by the cor anglais, an always penetrating, rising chromatic motif from the violas and cellos (*Una macchia*), and falling chromaticism. All these motifs have narrow intervals, short phrases, *sotto voce*, ambiguity of harmony and compulsive repetition. The song develops as free declamation, and it is only when memory of the deed breaks through the haze of Lady Macbeth's consciousness that there are longer, expressive phrases. She is a broken woman who can no longer speak, so the only 'melody' in this scene is the moving lament from the overture, played by the cor anglais, clarinets and violins, but not sung. Lady Macbeth tries to repeat her gesture of power (*Banco è spento*) with its three-note figure to which she sang in the second act of the *pleasure* of power, but the impossibly high note which the voice has to reach at the end (a high D flat) expresses her paralysis.

Verdi's operas were becoming popular abroad. The London season of 1847 opened with *Foscari*, playing simultaneously on two rival stages: Her Majesty's Theatre and Covent Garden. For some time Verdi had been receiving offers to compose an opera from Benjamin Lumley, the impresario at Her Majesty's, and so at the end of June he travelled north with his friend Emanuele Muzio through Switzerland, Germany, Belgium, France, and finally to England. Muzio recorded his first impressions in his diary: 'What chaos in London! What a hustle and bustle. Paris is nothing by comparison. People shouting, poor people crying, clouds of smoke in the air, people on horseback, in coaches, on foot and all screaming like the damned.'[42] For his part Verdi was fascinated by this *magnificent city*, at that time the largest in the world, although the climate did not suit him: he complained about the *fog* and the *smoke*, which *suffocated* him, and the constant *smell of coal* made him feel as if he was *on board a steamer*.[43] He hardly went out, and not just because of the language barrier and the dreadful wine: there were only about three weeks left until the first piano rehearsals and he had just begun to compose *I masnadieri*. It was based on *Die Räuber* (1781), a play by the German dramatist and poet Friedrich Schiller (1759–1805). *I masnadieri* was Verdi's second opera to a text by Schiller, the first being *Giovanna d'Arco*, inspired by Schiller's play about Joan of Arc, *Die Jungfrau von Orleans* (1801).

On 22 July 1847 the première of Verdi's only opera written for London was attended by Queen Victoria; and afterwards Muzio

Friedrich Schiller (1759–1805) was, with Johann Wolfgang von Goethe, the most famous and influential German dramatist, poet and historian. As the main representative of the Romantic *Sturm und Drang* movement his early works concern the desire for political and individual freedom and other ideals of the Enlightenment.

sent the following news to Busseto: 'They threw flowers and all you could hear was "Evviva Verdi! Bietifol!"'[44] Having the famous Swedish soprano Jenny Lind (1820–87) sing the part of Amalia was almost a guarantee of public success. Although I masnadieri was not taken into the repertory, with this contract Verdi was able to claim about four times the fee he would have been able to earn in Italy.

Four months later he made his debut at the Paris Opéra. Although it was the highest honour for an opera composer to write for the Opéra, it made a bad impression on Verdi. It seemed to him like a kind of *affreuse boutique*,[45] a *terrible shop*, with *dreadful* singers and an *at best average* orchestra.[46] The rehearsals, which extended over two months, were exhausting. *An opera at the Opéra is a strain that would fell an ox* he once complained during the composition of *Les vêpres siciliennes*.[47] In order to compete with the popular composers in France such as Auber, Halévy, and particularly Meyerbeer, Verdi took great trouble with *Jérusalem*, the new French version of I Lombardi. He removed the conventional chorus opening, the violin solo in the third act, and the rather banal pilgrim's tune. Paying great attention to the instrumentation, he wrote a new prelude, several new numbers, and the obligatory ballet, without which no opera in Paris was complete. Giuseppina Strepponi aided him in his work. The text, by the two librettists at the Opéra, Alphonse Royer and Gustave Vaëz, was better written than that of I Lombardi. It was less complicated, with more historical credibility, and in the finale of the third act it had an unusual execution scene. Set formal numbers were still

The German composer Giacomo Meyerbeer (1791–1864), was much admired by Verdi, who waxed lyrical over 'the power of Meyerbeer's genius'. He studied composition with Clementi and the Abbe Vogler. His position as the pre-eminent French composer of grand opera was established with the première of *Robert le diable* in 1831. Initially friendly with Wagner, he supported him financially; when the two fell out Wagner vented his anti-semitic vitriol at him. His longest opera, *L'Africane*, took 25 years to write.

Daniel Francois Esprit Auber (1782–1871) was recognised by Cherubini in Paris, where he had 45 operas produced between 1813 and 1869. The premiere of his *Maisonello, ou La Muette de Portici,* at the Opéra-Comique in 1829 was a historic event, stirring its audiences in France and Belgium to insurrection. He was appointed director of the Paris Conservatoire in 1842 by Louis Philippe, and did not leave the city during its siege by the Germans in 1870. He died during the Paris Commune.

common practice, as is evident from the ease with which arias and duets could be substituted and their order changed, or be furnished with new texts.

At that time, however, opera lovers in Paris were waiting expectantly for Meyerbeer's new opera *Le Prophète,* and this may be the reason why the first performance of Verdi's *Jérusalem* in November 1847 was only a moderate success. The takings were good, but the critics were reserved in their comments. Compared to Meyerbeer's *Les Huguenots* (1836) and *Robert le diable,* with Halévy's *La Juive* (1835), or Auber's *Masaniello ou La muette de Portici* (1828), people found Verdi's opera cumbersome and artificial, even a little dull.

While in Paris Verdi waited impatiently for news of home. An economic crisis had led to growing resistance to Metternich's system, although the leaders of the opposition groups were

Influenced by Mazzini, the Italian soldier Giuseppe Garibaldi (1807–82) joined an attempted republican revolution in Sardinia-Piedmont in 1834 and was forced to flee to South America. He returned to join the Revolution of 1848. After another period of exile he supported the unification movement led by Cavour and Victor Emmanuel II of Sardinia-Piedmont. In 1860 he set out from Genoa on the Expedition of a Thousand, achieving the conquest of Sicily and Naples. He also fought for the French in the Franco-Prussian War (1870–1).

still in exile: Guiseppe Mazzini, who wanted a republic, as did Verdi; Giuseppe Garibaldi, who had joined Mazzini; and Vincenzo Gioberti, who took the more moderate line of founding a constitutional monarchy.

The hope uniting them all was that national unity would bring liberation. Since the change in the pontificate in 1846 great hopes were being placed on Pope Pius IX, a known liberal who had won such sympathy with his amnesty for political prisoners that during a performance of *Ernani* in 1847 in Rome, the chorus of homage to Charles V was transformed into a demonstration for the new Pope, as they sang 'Pio Nono' in place of 'Carlo Quinto'.

A Pi - o No-no sia glo-ria ed o - nor!

An unsuccessful uprising in Messina in September 1847 was the trigger, and there were disturbances in Milan during the same month. At the end of the year a new journal appeared, which gave its name to the whole nationalist movement: Il *Risorgimento* ('Resurgence'). Its most important contributor was Camillo di Cavour.

In March 1848 there were uprisings in Palermo, Venice and other cities. For five days (the *cinque giornate*) the citizens of Milan fought the Austrian army at the barricades. When Verdi returned there in April the Austrians had been driven out of the city. A provisional government had been formed under Gabrio Casati, and Mazzini and other members of the resistance had returned from exile. *I am intoxicated with joy*, wrote Verdi to Private Piave, who was now serving in the Venetian Guard. *Honour these brave men! Honour the whole of Italy, which has*

Italian statesman Count Camillo Benso di Cavour (1810–61) unified Italy in 1861. He formed his first government in 1852 under Victor Emmanuel II of Sardinia-Piedmont. Cavour accepted an alliance with France and Britain during the Crimean War and agreed a further alliance with France in 1859 to remove Austria from Italy. He resigned when France came to terms with Austria but became Prime Minister again in 1860, arranging the union of Sardinia-Piedmont with Parma, Modena, Tuscany, and the Romagna.

Victor Emmanuel II (1820–78) was King of Italy from 1861 to 1878. He fought the Austrians and co-operated with Garibaldi in the campaign that freed Southern Italy. As King of Italy he acquired Venetia (1866) and Rome (1870), which he made the capital.

The Risorgimento (Resurgence) is the name given to the nationalist movement in 19th-century Italy which achieved the country's independence and unification. Beginning with clandestine meetings and popular uprisings, it achieved success in 1859 when the Piedmontese Prime Minister, Cavour, freed Lombardy from Austrian rule. In 1860 Garibaldi surrendered to Piedmont his conquests made in Tuscany, Modena, Parma, Bologna, and Romagna, and accepted entry into the kingdom of Italy under the House of Piedmont, proclaimed in 1861. Unification was complete when Italy took Venetia in 1866 and the Papal States in 1870.

become truly great! The hour of freedom has struck, of that we can be sure. It is the will of the people: And if it is the will of the people, then there is no power that can resist them . . . Yes, indeed, a few more years, maybe only months, and Italy will be free, united, a republic.[48]

But it was not to be. Following an offensive by Radetzky's army, against which the Piedmont troops of King Charles Albert and partisans under Garibaldi fought in vain, the old rulers had been reinstated by the middle of August. *Italy? My poor country!!!* wrote Verdi from Paris. Although he was one of the signatories of a letter to the French General Cavaignac, appealing for help from France, he told Clara Maffei that his only hope was for civil unrest within Austria itself. *France*, he reluctantly concluded, *does not wish to see Italy become a nation.*[49] The hymn *Suona la tromba*, which he sent to Mazzini in October, came too late *to be sung on the plains of Lombardy.*[50]

By May 1848 Verdi was corresponding with Salvatore Cammarano, the librettist at the Teatro San Carlo in Naples, about a patriotic opera. Cammarano wrote a libretto based on the defence of Lombardy against the Emperor Frederick Barbarossa. *La battaglia*

Naples' Teatro San Carlo, the social hub of the city, was opened in 1737, and enlarged twice in the ensuing 70 years. In 1816 it burned down, and was rebuilt in only six months. Donizetti, Bellini, Mercadante and Verdi all had operas premièred in this extraordinary theatre.

di Legnano had its first performance on 27 January 1849 in the Teatro Argentina in Rome. The hymn of the Lombard League, *Viva Italia* – with which the opera opens, and which runs like a

1813	The former Duchy of Parma is conquered by Napoleon I and becomes part of France.
1814–15	The Congress of Vienna. The situation prior to the French Revolution is restored. Austrian rule is re-established in Italy. The Habsburg Maria Luigia becomes Duchess of Parma.
1830	Uprisings in Italy following the July Revolution in Paris are put down by Austria.
1848	Uprisings in many parts of the country against foreign rule. Sardinia-Piedmont becomes a permanent constitutional state. In the first war of independence it is against Austria, but remains at the centre of the National movement.
1859	Sardinia-Piedmont and France declare war on Austria, which loses Lombardy to Piedmont, but retains Venetia.
1860	A public plebiscite in the Italian states leads to unity with Sardinia-Piedmont.
1861	The first Italian Parliament proclaims Victor Emmanuel II as King of Italy.
1866	Austria cedes Venetia to France, which 'hands' it to Italy.
1870	The Papal State joins the union. Rome becomes the capital city.

motto through all four acts – two scenes in which ceremonial oaths are sworn, and finally the chorus *Italia risorge* ('Italy rises again') so appealed to the patriotism of the audience that the whole of the third act had to be repeated. The Italians' *holy war* against their *rapacious, red-haired* German opponents, that *horde of barbarians*, chimed exactly with the predominant mood in Rome; and Rome (as well as Venice) was the one bastion of nationalist resistance that could be successfully defended. Shortly before the proclamation of the Republic of Rome on 9 February 1849, people were keen to hear their own aims expressed and Verdi was happy to oblige: *He who dies for his Fatherland cannot have such guilt in his heart* intone the chorus and soloists in the final scene of *La battaglia di Legnano*, accompanied by arpeggios on the harp. With his final words – *Italy is saved* – the dying hero voiced all the audience's hopes and aspirations. But then, six months later, these hopes were dashed when the Pope and the former rulers were reinstated, with help from France. *The situation in our country is hopeless!* Verdi lamented. *Italy is nothing more that a huge and beautiful prison . . . Paradise for the eyes, but Hell for the heart!*[51]

He remained in Paris for almost two years, although he disliked the boulevards and the fashionable society life led by his friend, the soprano Giuseppina Strepponi. Although they lived not far from one another, and saw each other regularly, Verdi never mentions her in his letters. After the devastation caused by the revolution of 1848 they both moved into a house in Passy, close to the city. Verdi was especially glad to escape from his many duties and pressures, for he could at last enjoy a little privacy. *It is a great pleasure to do as one likes!!!*[52] In the finale of the second act of *Jérusalem* (the dialogue between the lovers), the autograph score is in Giuseppina Strepponi's handwriting as well as Verdi's. She wrote the words for Gaston while Verdi wrote Hélène's, and implicit in the score is a promise that would last until Giuseppina's death:

GASTON: *My fame is fled! Family . . . Fatherland . . . I have lost everything!*
HÉLÈNE: *No! I will stay with you for the rest of my life!*

In the summer of 1849 Giuseppina Strepponi went to Florence to arrange an apprenticeship for her son Camillo with the sculptor Lorenzo Bartolini. Verdi had gone to live in the Palazzo Cavalli in Busseto and had daringly invited Giuseppina to stay with him there. But in case country life might bore her he tentatively offered to have her taken wherever she might wish to go. 'Good heavens!' she replied. 'Have people in Busseto forgotten how to be kind and how to write with feeling?' She added that she would like everything, absolutely everything. 'Just so long as you are there, you silly old monster.'[53]

'Bold Subject Matter – Bold in the Extreme' · 1849–1853

The first floor of the Palazzo Cavalli, with its loggia looking out on a little inner courtyard, had large and lavishly furnished rooms, but life was lonely in these imposing surroundings. The ambiguous relationship between Verdi and this lady from Paris provided the provincial town with ample material for *gossip, rumours*, and *disapproval*.[54] He and Giuseppina Strepponi lived a retiring life and they had no guests apart from Antonio and Giovanni Barezzi. Verdi

The present-day Palazzo Orlandi on the main street in Busseto was known as the Palazzo Cavalli when Verdi bought it in 1845. It had belonged to the Mayor of Busseto. The rooms were hardly suited to the modest and retiring lifestyle of Verdi and Giuseppina at that time.

avoided social contacts, thereby offending many people who thought Busseto deserved better from its famous composer. *What harm is there*, Verdi wrote to his father-in-law, *if I decide not to pay calls on titled people? If I do not take part in festivities, or the recreations of other people? If I look after my property because that is what I like doing and what gives me pleasure: I repeat: Where is the harm in this?*[55]

Giuseppina kept herself so far out of the public eye that people did not know what her relationship with Verdi really was, and this gave rise to whispering campaigns. Now homesick for Paris, Verdi sent thousands of questions to his French publisher, Escudier, and grumbled about provincial life. Giuseppina, who felt as though she were a prisoner in a convent cell, found the general contempt of the townspeople towards her hard to bear. For devout Catholics (like Verdi's parents) a relationship without the blessing of the church was scandalous, and Giuseppina was therefore unfit for polite society, to say nothing of her dubious reputation. A Catholic herself, it is probable that Giuseppina was unable to attend Mass. All this made Verdi very bitter about his *charming home town: How wonderful! How elegant! What a place! What society!*[56]

In October 1849 he travelled to Naples with Barezzi for the first rehearsals of his new opera *Luisa Miller* in the Teatro San Carlo. Salvatore Cammarano had reduced Schiller's family tragedy to a suitable libretto for an opera, editing out the portrayal of social hierarchy and the analysis of power structures. Verdi regretted that Lady Milford had to become an insignificant duchess, but he went along with this plot since he had confidence in Cammarano.

The subject matter of *Luisa Miller* differed from the composer's patriotic operas in that it emphasised the moral stance of the individual rather than the rights of a people or a state. Its portrayal of individual conflict appears more true to life than the political operas with their choral declarations. The ability of the music to delineate character is shown in Miller, another of Verdi's father figures, who witnesses the destruction of all the values he holds dear. He is first presented as a naive and upright soldier, proud of his honour, in the lively cabaletta (*Ah! fu giusto*). But in his duet with Luisa, when fear and horror induce feelings of giddiness, his soldier's honour counts for nothing. The semi-chromatic, oscillating, downward motif in the strings allows us to hear the ground moving beneath Miller's feet.

In Luisa (the first of Verdi's protagonists to come from a modest family background) Verdi reveals the inability of the individual to escape from those in power. This is what links her with Gilda, Violetta, Amelia, Leonora, Elisabeth, and eventually Aida. The impossibility of experiencing love in the real world becomes a paradigm for insuperable social barriers. Desires and hopes are expressed in arias, in duets, in prayers, in which, for a brief moment, the longed-for happiness is attained or experienced in a vision. It is clear that Luisa is a prisoner right from the overture, with its brief and restless melody in a minor mode that continues to the end. It reappears as a reminder in various guises throughout the opera, in connection with enforced actions such as the writing of the letter. When in the first act the offstage hunting chorus repeat *The catch is ours, it cannot escape* just at the moment when Luisa learns she has been deceived, it becomes a cynical commentary on her plight. The a cappella quartet in the second act is a good example of how the music points up the gulf between the individual and society. While the voices of the others are singing in strict time in G major, Luisa sings in G minor, with syncopation and wide deviations from the regular beat. Her andantino from the duet with Miller (*La tomba è un letto*) provides a stark contrast to the overture's motif of coercion and fear of death. Here is a song about death in which *the heavens open* for love, to be sung pianissimo, *lightly, quite gently*, almost like a dance, a vision of happiness in which all obstacles are overcome.

The première in Naples on 8 December 1849 was a success, but matters at home in Busseto took a turn for the worse. Animosity from various new quarters, difficult negotiations with the Teatro La Fenice (which, like most other opera houses, was in financial difficulties following the revolution), plus a heavy cold combined to make Verdi extremely irritable. Naturally Peppina (as Giuseppina was fondly known) had to bear the brunt of all his moods. In June a storm ruined the fruit harvest and the vines. At the end of the year a thoroughly bad performance of *Gerusalemme*, the Italian version of *Jérusalem*, at La Scala, caused yet further irritation. Then, in January 1851, there was a quarrel between Verdi and his father. Carlo Verdi had been looking after the estate, although he had little experience and so had got into debt. This led to a break between Verdi and his parents, who were obliged to leave their home in Sant'Agata and move at very short notice to a tiny house in the neighbouring Vidalenza. Verdi insisted on a legal separation of the rights *to the house and the business*[57] and engaged a lawyer with instructions that his decision was *irrevocable*, because he was *tired of the scenes* which his father was *continually* making. In June, while the quarrel – which Verdi described as *painful* and *shameful* – was still going on, his mother died. 'Peppina hates to see him cry,' Muzio reported. 'He never wants to leave home again.'[58] Verdi was reconciled with his father.

For the first time Verdi had two contracts simultaneously, one with the Teatro La Fenice and one with the Teatro Grande in Trieste, so he immersed himself more deeply than ever in his work. He wanted to find his own individual musical voice, to express himself *in a completely new manner, not bound by the traditions of opera*,[59] and he looked at the most varied source material – plays by Byron, Victor Hugo, the Austrian dramatist Franz Grillparzer (1791–1872), Jean Racine (1639–99), the Italian Vittorio Alfieri (1749–1803), and Shakespeare once again, not only *King Lear* (1604–5), but

Hamlet (1602) and *The Tempest* (1611). In the end he settled on a contemporary subject (a new departure for him). *Stiffelio* was based on *Le Pasteur* (1849) by Eugène Bourgeois and Emile Souvestre. A marital drama with a middle-class Protestant setting, its protagonist, a middle-aged pastor, was the very antithesis of a traditional opera hero. The censor required sweeping changes, but *Stiffelio* had its first performance in Trieste in November 1850.

In April that year Verdi discovered a text by Victor Hugo which he loved: *Oh, 'Le Roi s'amuse'* [1832] *is the most marvellous material, maybe the greatest modern drama!* he wrote. He asked Piave to start negotiations immediately with Marzari in Venice. Piave came to stay in Verdi's house and they worked together for two months, first on the libretto for *Stiffelio* and then on the play by Hugo on which *Rigoletto* was based. The police ban on this new project came at the very last minute and was so unexpected that Verdi *almost went out of my mind.*[60] Marzari, who had been hoping that the first performance of an opera by the famous composer would considerably ease La Fenice's finances, tried to rescue the opera by making extensive changes to the libretto. Verdi read the butchered text with horror. Everything that might be considered offensive, cruel, or violent had been removed. The censors found the last scene to be in the worst taste: Rigoletto discovers it is not the Duke but his dying daughter he has been dragging in a sack to the river. *It is vital that the Duke is a libertine,* Verdi insisted in his defence, otherwise the curse, *which is so terrible and magnificent in the original, will become ludicrous. I do not understand why the sack was taken out! Why did the sack matter to the police? Were they worried about the effect it might have? Permit me then to ask: why do they think they know more about it than I do? Who is the maestro here?* He could cope with changes of name, period, and place, but he was horrified that Rigoletto might no longer be a hunchback: *I think it is splendid to put on stage a character who is deformed and ridiculous, yet at the same time passionate* and loving. I chose the subject for just these very qualities and original features. If they are suppressed I can no longer set it to music. If they tell me that my music will fit the new text just as well, then I shall reply that I do not understand their argument, and I have to say honestly that I never just compose my music at random, whether it be good or bad, but I always endeavour to give it character.[61] In January 1851 Piave sent news that the opera had finally been approved 'without disruptions and mutilations'.[62] Verdi had won.

In *Rigoletto* the vivacious music for the dance in the *magnificent hall* of the ducal palace, which runs throughout the first scene, is in many ways a façade. It seems out of place after the prelude, where the 'curse' motif predicts a catastrophe. False names and attitudes, masks and disguises demonstrate the general hypocrisy, and the dance music points this up. The lightly veiled aggression of the courtiers is set against a crude galop for the banda. The dialogue during the ball music is about gossip, treachery, and intimidation, while a rococo style of minuet (a reference to Mozart's *Don Giovanni*) provides a gallant mask for the Duke's indiscretions. After the courtiers have planned their revenge, everyone celebrates in a fast, wild chorus (*Tutto è gioia*). The celebrations are rudely interrupted, however, by Monterone, a victim of the Duke's licentiousness. As he names the injustice done to him and curses the Duke and his adviser, Rigoletto, he instils terror in them all, just like the Commendatore in *Don Giovanni*. Fear and repressed anger are heard in a chorus sung *sotto voce*, but it is Rigoletto alone who is silenced in horror.

Rigoletto is a victim of self-deception. He believes that the individual can somehow preserve his integrity by submitting to external authority, while defending his own private world. This blindness is the curse – *La maledizione* as the opera was originally to be called. The curse is neither magical nor supernatural, and it applies only to Rigoletto, not to the Duke, who is immune to moral scruples. The memory of Monterone's curse, from which Rigoletto cannot free himself, arouses little more than a dim premonition of the hopelessness of his life, shown by the constantly varied repetition of its terse theme. He tries to escape the hateful world and his misfortune by adopting many different faces, leading to his own deformity, his hunchback and his jester's costume. *La rà, la rà* is his sad attempt to imitate the tone of the courtiers adopting the march rhythm of their mocking comments (*scorrendo uniti*). He serves the Duke, encourages him in his violence, imitates Monterone cynically offering the victim 'clemency', all of which shows how his desire for acceptance has driven him to despise society. Woodwind motifs, with their sharply accented rhythms and bizarre leaps, reveal his duplicity and at the same time the violence behind his disguise. His aggressiveness is also clear from the cabaletta of his duet with Gilda in the second act (*Si, vendetta*), a joyful expression of revenge, whose extremes are illustrated by the forced sound of the trumpet in the postlude.

His fervent plea for Gilda's safety in the duet *Ah! veglia, o donna,* with its expressive syncopated accents, reveals the voice of the *other man*. Rigoletto believes that his daughter Gilda embodies the essence of life itself, *religion, family, home*. He sees her as the Madonna in paradise. *Here I become another person* he sings as he enters his house, and although this gentle passage with its solo flute accompaniment is just one small episode in a monologue filled with hatred and pain, it demonstrates the fragility of his 'paradise'. Evidence of how music can present a psychological portrait can be heard in Rigoletto's aria in the second act: when he suppresses his agitation behind his jester's mask in his *La rà*; when he upbraids the courtiers, in the incessant sextuplets for the strings; and when he eventually drops his guard, begging his tormentors for mercy. In the third act, immediately before his downfall, Rigoletto starts a final song of revenge, beginning in a grand way, breaking off,

LA DONNA È MOBILE

beginning again, interrupted by the clock striking midnight, then, instead of a great triumphant aria, the Duke's *canzone* is suddenly heard. *La donna è mobile* settles in the listener's ear like a popular song, with its simple phrases, dancing triple beat, and its predictable bass, as it celebrates how partners are interchangeable, and at the same time provides a mocking commentary on Rigoletto's blindness.

By his own admission, Verdi composed the opera *as an endless sequence of duets*,[63] making less use of large ensembles and set-piece arias with chorus. In this way he heightened the conflict between the characters, who now stand out as unmistakable individuals, and express themselves in new, unusual ways. The quartet in the third act is a good example of how each voice maintains its own method of expression within an ensemble. They each express their very different feelings simultaneously, in such a way that the combination makes an aesthetic whole: the Duke's wooing flattery, echoed in the music; Maddalena's laughter in her coquettish staccato response; Rigoletto's threats, in semitones, and finally Gilda's lament for her lost love, in long notes, full of pain, until, in her mounting agitation, her faltering breath interrupts both words and melody (this is a *melodia spezzata*, a melodic line broken by frequent pauses).

The dramatic climax is reached in the storm scene of the finale. It begins like a dance of death with open fifths and the strangled sound of the oboe suggesting the eventual outcome. The three-note figures for the flutes and the string tremolos not only illustrate thunder and lightning but also combine with the voices to present the drama as it unfolds. The chromatic humming chorus, used like an orchestral instrument, creates a completely new musical effect, the natural force of all those who suffer and are tormented. At the very end, however, Gilda's gentle singing, accompanied by flute and violin arpeggios, presents in both its harmony and its sound a

Sant'Agata. *Four walls for protection against the sun and the ravages of the elements; a couple of dozen trees, most of which I have planted myself, and a swamp, which I will dignify with the name of 'lake' when I have enough water to fill it, etc. etc. No plans for any of it, no architectural design.*[64]

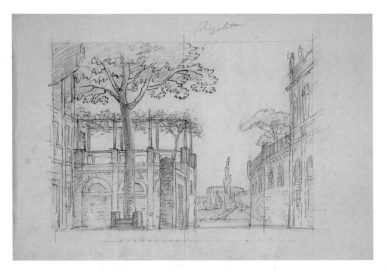

Sketch of the stage set for the first performance of *Rigoletto* at the Teatro La Fenice in Venice on 11 March 1851.

completely different world, indicating the end of violence, hatred, and despair in a vision of reconciliation. Verdi used almost exactly the same phrase in *Il trovatore* (Act 1, Scene 2), when Leonora remembers 'the stuff of an airy dream' (*Come d'aurato sogno fuggente imago!*).

The first performance of *Rigoletto* on 11 March 1851 – with Felice Varesi, Teresa Brambilla and Raffaele Mirate – was Verdi's greatest success so far. The critics particularly praised the quartet and the instrumentation, and it soon entered the repertoire of opera houses abroad.

In May 1851 Verdi and Giuseppina moved to the villa of Sant'Agata, near Villanova d'Arda. It had taken almost a decade of constant renovation and rebuilding to transform this simple farm into an elegant country house, and a period of unaccustomed peace and solitude now began.

The nearest village was half a kilometre away, and it was three kilometres to Busseto. The roads were impassable after heavy rain and the River Ongina flooded every spring. They had to cross the river by a narrow wooden bridge to reach the house, and there were times when they seemed to be surrounded by water, mists, and mud. Apart from the Barezzis, Piave was one of their few guests in the first years. Giuseppina found the winter months especially oppressive, when the house became even more isolated by the snow. She hung flowery curtains in the windows to hide the 'bleak skeletons' of the trees, because it seemed so 'sad, silent, and bare' outside. Verdi, however, with his 'iron nature', loved the countryside in winter.[65] At first he complained of being *surrounded by farmers and oxen*, but he soon found his new life 'a revelation', as Giuseppina confided to the Countess Maffei.[66] At the beginning of March 1854, when Clara Maffei asked him if he would not like to 'take root' in Paris, Verdi replied: *That is impossible. I love my wilderness and my sky too much.*[67] In the summer, Giuseppina enjoyed 'the healthy air and sunshine'. She was particularly fond of the garden with its many flowers, trees, and birds. To begin with it was always known as 'Peppina's Garden', but when it grew larger Verdi ruled it 'like a little czar'.[68]

It was Verdi who gradually transformed Sant'Agata into a model estate. He worked hard and passionately – not only at musical composition. He was also very knowledgeable about farming and vine-growing, experimenting with new varieties of wheat and grapes. He soon knew a great deal about breeding cattle and horses too, learning from his farmhands. He acted as architect for countless building projects and studied irrigation in order to water his vegetable fields from the River Ongina. 'The farmers worship him,' his French publisher Escudier noted after a visit.[69] At the cattle market in Cremona they could spot Verdi from a long way off by his wide-brimmed hat. He was happy to stop and talk to them when he was inspecting his fields, sometimes on horseback, often out on long walks with his little Maltese dog, Loulou, under his coat or a book in his hand. He recovered so well that Giuseppina reported in 1858 that he was now in 'such rude health and had such a tan that he could well go to the colonies and plant sugar-cane'.[70] In December 1851 they left their 'cave', as she called the estate, and spent three months in Paris, where *Macbeth* and *Luisa Miller* were being performed in French. Verdi was contracted to compose a work for the Opéra, although *Les vêpres siciliennes* was not to be performed until some years later in the summer of 1855.

In Paris Verdi received a letter from his father-in-law which contained *some very hurtful words*. For some reason Barezzi, who had been obliged to listen to all sorts of things being said about Verdi in Busseto, felt that he had been disregarded. Verdi replied to him in an unusually long and explicit letter:

Antonio Barezzi. *You know that I owe him everything, absolutely everything,* Verdi wrote to Clara Maffei shortly before Barezzi's death. *This loss will be grievous for me!*[71]

In my house there lives a free and independent lady who loves solitude, as I do, and who has her own financial means which shelter her from need. Neither she nor I need account to anyone for our actions; and what is more, who is to know what the relationship between us may be? What business arrangements? What ties? What claims I have on her and she on me? Who knows whether she is my wife or not? And who knows what particular reasons we may have in this case for not making the matter public? Who knows if that is a good thing or a bad one? Why should it not be a good thing? And even if it were a bad one, who has the right to ostracise us? What I can say is that in my house she should be granted the same respect as I enjoy, perhaps more even, and no one should forget it, for whatever reason; and that she has a perfect right to this on account of her behaviour, her intellect, and on account of the particular consideration which she never fails to show to others.[72]

Some time later Verdi complained to Clara Maffei of his deep depression following his return from Paris: *A dreadfully rapid sequence of troubles and misfortunes has befallen me recently. I, who would give anything for a little peace and quiet, and do everything I can to find it, am unable to do so. I travel the world, from the tumult of the city to the almost empty countryside, but it is all in vain.*[73] He had been urging Cammarano to finish the libretto for the new opera, since time was *extremely important.*[74] For the first time it was not a commissioned opera, but a more personal project that Verdi had been working on for a year. Cammarano, however, was ill. (He had been in dire straits since the Revolution, as the San Carlo opera house had not paid his salary for months, despite urgent reminders.) The news of his death in July 1852 caught Verdi completely unawares, and he sent a sum of money to the widow and six children. It was left to a young Venetian librettist, Leone Emanuele Bardare, to complete Cammarano's work on the opera, which was to be called *Il trovatore* (*The Troubadour*).

It became the quintessential Italian opera. *If you were to travel to India, or to Central Africa, you would be able to hear the Troubadour,* Verdi wrote to a friend in 1862.[75] It has remained one of his most popular operas, with its effective bel canto numbers and its unison choruses, despite the fact that the libretto is extremely muddled. Scenes out of their logical sequence, individual moments isolated from the action of the plot, brief flashbacks, eight contrasting scenes, all these are part of the aesthetic of *romanticismo*. For instance, the decisive events that occur between the first and second acts – the brothers' duel and later a battle between their troops – are revealed only in retrospect and almost incidentally. This romanticisation of the Middle Ages pays little heed either to continuity or historical accuracy, so the opera includes gypsies, troubadours, and the burning of witches – all complete anachronisms in 1400.

The important elements here are the ballad-like effect of fantastic events, the vividness and the diversity of the scenes. Inspired by Victor Hugo's stated aims in his *Préface to 'Cromwell'*, Verdi had sought to bring life in all its variety on to the stage as Shakespeare – 'that God of the theatre' – had done; and in so doing to tear down 'the dilapidated house of pedantry', as Hugo called it. One of Hugo's followers was Antonio García y Gutiérrez, the 23-year-old Spanish author of the play *El Trovador*, on which Cammarano and Bardare's libretto was based, and which perfectly answered Verdi's desire for *new, original, unique* and *bizarre* material. Verdi's principle of *varietà*, of melodic diversity and contrasting

Stage set by Girolamo Magnani for Act 1 of *Il Trovatore* at a performance in Parma in 1853. – By moonlight in the palace gardens a troubadour sang a mournful song. Leonora: Cavatina, Act 1, Scene 2.

means of expression, and the extravagant profusion of the melodies themselves, are an attempt to reflect this diversity of life in music. For Hugo and his school, the scene of the action should be a 'sort of silent witness' without which the drama would be incomplete, so *Il trovatore* contains backgrounds typical of Gothic horror: a castle with a haunted roof; an unknown nocturnal troubadour singing in the palace gardens; a gypsy camp at night; the cloister of a convent; a military encampment; a dark dungeon in a tower. The mystery of Manrico's birth picks up a motif from *Nabucco* (Abigaille) and *Rigoletto* (Gilda), and recurs again in *Les vêpres siciliennes* (Henri).

The motif of the feuding brothers reflects a society dominated by revenge rather than justice. In the final act, the transience of life – the tolling bell, a miserere, and a funeral march – is the background against which the lovers sing together, thus characterising the hopelessness of this world, in which Leonora's sacrificial death is as senseless as Luna's revenge exacted on his own brother. The gypsy Azucena, traumatised by the death of her mother at

The flame motif (*Stride la vampa*) returns twice in the orchestra, the jaggedness of the melodic line portraying the flames.

the stake, and suffering terrible visions of madness, represents all victims who are denied justice. The jagged rhythms and leaps in her melodies portray the flames that she thinks pursue her, and the

STRIDE LA VAMPA

German composer Richard Wagner (1813–83) changed the course of western music. His early operas *Rienzi* (1842) and *Der fliegende Holländer* (*The Flying Dutchman*, 1843) led to his appointment as conductor at the Dresden opera house, where *Tannhäuser* (1845) was successfully performed. He began a project for a series of operas based on German mythology, the Nibelungen sagas. His influential long essay *Oper und Drama* (*Opera and Drama*, 1850–1) expounds his theory of musical drama. While composing *Der Ring des Nibelungen* (*The Nibelung's Ring*) he had an affair with a married woman which inspired his opera *Tristan und Isolde* (1857–9). He later married Liszt's daughter, Cosima, who had been married to the long-suffering Hans von Bülow (1837–1930). In 1868 he produced *Die Meistersinger von Nürnberg* (*The Mastersingers of Nuremberg*) and began building a theatre in Bayreuth for the first complete performance (1876) of the *Ring* cycle. His last opera, *Parsifal*, was produced in Bayreuth in 1882. From 1878 he suffered a series of heart attacks, the last one, in Venice, proving fatal. In 1875, Cosima wrote in her diary 'In the evening, Verdi's Requiem, about which it would be best to say nothing.'

persistently repeated note indicates her obsession. In Act 2, when her song (*Condotto ell'era in ceppi* [Act 2, Scene 5]) breaks the ballad form, it stands in stark contrast to the arias and duets of the other characters, whose more typically operatic feelings are expressed in the usual forms. Verdi accommodated himself here, against his better judgement, to his experienced librettist, as can be seen from a sentence in his letter of 4 April 1851 to Cammarano, in which he expresses an idea similar to Wagner's own at this time: *If in opera there were no cavatinas, no duets, no trios, no choruses or grand finales etc., and if a whole opera (I might almost say) could consist in a single unit, then I would find this more reasonable and proper.*[77]

A measure of Verdi's fame at this point can be seen not only in the fact that he was awarded the Cross of the Legion of Honour but also that he was approached by the first of his biographers, Luzatti. Verdi gave his permission for a biography rather half-heartedly, on condition that Luzatti should most definitely not overlook the role of the clerics who tried to prevent his installation as music master in Busseto. Verdi never overcame his dislike of priests, and he irreverently named two of his dogs Pretin ('little priest') and Prevost ('provost'). Luzatti's project came to grief since Verdi changed his mind, and the task fell instead to Giuseppe Demaldè from Busseto, a longtime friend of the composer, who assembled the first biographical work, the *Cenni biografici del Maestro Verdi*.

At the beginning of January 1853, even before the première of *Il trovatore*, Verdi was telling his friend Cesare De Sanctis about a new and completely different project:

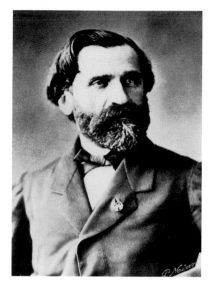

Verdi wearing the Cross of the Legion of Honour, c.1870.

I am doing the Lady of the Camelias in Venice, which may be entitled 'Traviata'. It is a contemporary piece. Other composers might perhaps not have undertaken it out of moral scruples, or because of the period, or a thousand other ludicrous reasons.[77]

It is probable that he and Giuseppina had seen the play by Alexandre Dumas (*fils*), *La dame aux camélias* (1852), at the Vaudeville Theatre in Paris. Although Verdi knew that contemporary themes were not popular for an opera, and that the choice of a courtesan as protagonist might not go down well with the audience, he insisted on *bold subject matter, bold in the extreme.*[78] No doubt the gossip and snubs he had endured in Busseto had a bearing on his choice of subject and found their way into the work. There is an element of defiance in the cautious realism of *La traviata* (*The Fallen Woman*), with its frequent mention of money, and the way in which possessions and bourgeois attitudes play a decisive part in

Caricatures of Verdi by Melchiorre Delfico. Verdi wrote to Piave in 1853: *You know that I have not gone searching for anyone to write my biography, and that they have always disgusted me in the extreme.*[79]

the action rather than hiding in the background. Nevertheless, Violetta's ordeals and her gradual isolation in an unfeeling society, are presented with aesthetic detachment, while her misery, poverty, and illness seem somewhat stylised. *La traviata* is neither strictly realistic nor autobiographical. But Verdi's remarkably subdued comments and his laconic messages to his friends show how upset he was at the failure of the first performance. He avoided reference in his conversations and letters to the themes of love and death, which had inspired him to find new expression in his music. It was as if he had put them aside as forbidden subjects for the time being.

In *La traviata* every scene takes place indoors. In contrast to all his earlier operas, the dramatic action is concentrated on one single figure, Violetta, whose vocal part far overshadows all the others. She represents the image of the feminine widely held in the nineteenth century – a fragile woman with an exaggerated sensitivity and capacity for suffering – yet in her search for independence and freedom she seems thoroughly modern. Her joy in life, which drives her from *one round of pleasure to another*, can be heard in the waltzes, the *drinking song*, and especially in her *very brilliant* cabaletta (*Sempre libera*), a restless sequence of notes that repeatedly defers any pause in the music. The sequence of scenes presents sharp contrasts: disillusion follows idyll; Violetta's deepest humiliation occurs during a ball; the bacchanale and the death scene are juxtaposed. In the house in the country, which might be the setting for a *heavenly* life, according to Alfredo, there is no love duet. Instead, the action plunges suddenly into catastrophe with the confrontation between Violetta and Germont. Alfredo's father, defending a world that is fragmenting, fights for his family's social position and their possessions. Even when he clothes his demand in religious terms he is still exacting a sacrifice from Violetta, so that his own daughter should not lose her chance of happiness, for she has a position in society and is *as pure as an angel*. Germont shows how the musical characterisation of the father suffering for his children has developed, in comparison with Verdi's earlier operas. The strong orchestral motif heralding Germont's entrance immediately denotes his absolute authority, something that his son dare not question. When his first attempt to persuade Violetta fails, Germont the tactician is revealed in the way he uses her gratitude for his praise, repeating her tune (*Oh, come dolce*) for his own ends, as he is in the way in which he sings of the threat to his daughter's happiness *dolcissime,* with eloquent tied notes and appoggiaturas. The critical attitude of this character, the total absence of the customary heroic passion, turned Varesi completely against performing this role, although he had portrayed Macbeth and Rigoletto so convincingly.

Germont never loses face. The control with which he sings in A flat major, in a perfectly regular form, stands in sharp contrast to Violetta's agitated reply in C minor (*Vivacissimo, ancora più vivo*), a rushed sequence of notes twisting in all directions. She is fighting for her life. Germont's reaction to the constant repetition of her notes, to the desperate appeal of her highest notes, is callously to repeat his patronising phrase (*È grave il sagrifizio*): with the pathos of self-justification, he presents to us the view of an upright member of society in contrast to the dubious character of her so-called love. Violetta, however, is beyond lectures or comfort. When she comprehends the impossibility of her love in reality, her renunciation is sung as a variant of the love theme, a farewell, which she sings *da sè* ('to herself'), in a quite different harmonic realm, completely remote from Germont who, although he is not without sympathy for her situation, nevertheless eventually succeeds. Verdi himself considered that this duet was the best he had yet composed. The way in which the expression of feelings changes the prescribed form can be seen here in the reversal of the usual sequence, andante-allegro. The unequal struggle (*allegro*

moderato, vivacissimo) is followed by Violetta's submission, her quiet
E-flat major cantilena *andantino*. It is a crucial element of the opera
that Violetta cannot see that it is she who is being deceived: she
still clings to the illusion that her renunciation of love will allow her
to be accepted by this family in some way; she still regards herself
as guilty – as the *traviata*, the fallen woman or one who has gone
astray – and it is this element that is so touching.

The proximity of love and death – reflected in the early title *Amore
e morte* – is expressed in the music of the prelude. The very gentle

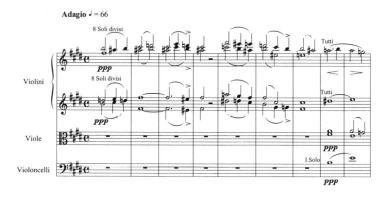

Prelude to *La traviata*. In the prelude to Alzira's dream Verdi had
already used the extreme tone colouring of violins divided in four
parts to characterise a completely different sphere. It is reminiscent of Wagner's instrumentation in the prelude to Wagner's
Lohengrin (1846–8), which Verdi did not know at this time.

chordal sequence played by divisi violins, which is associated with
Violetta's death, is followed by her love theme (*Amami, Alfredo*, Act
2, Scene 6), similar both in rhythm and in its falling movement to
the death music; and like the latter, with an interrupted cadence
after the seventh bar, again unresolved, so that this lack of resolu-
tion itself appears integral in the musical composition. Alfredo's

love theme, which recurs at dramatic points in all three acts, is so remarkably similar to Violetta's love theme, that it might be considered a variation, despite being more lively with its 3/8 movement and its soaring climax. Recurring themes and tone colours are some of the means Verdi used to create a musical unity in opera. It is only at the very end that Alfredo and the dying Violetta sing a love duet (*Parigi, o cara*). Their song of a future together is, however, like a lullaby with which to sing each other into a dream.[80] In place of the traditional final climax, their joint cadence is extremely quiet, a whispered evocation of happiness.

The garden gate at Sant'Agata. Verdi had begun to plant trees to celebrate certain operas: a plane tree for *Rigoletto*, an oak for *Il trovatore*, and a weeping willow for *La traviata*.

Verdi had a premonition of the fiasco to come while he was still working on the score and suffering rheumatic pains in his right arm. The combination of setting the action in the seventeenth century (a precautionary measure) with singers in brocade, curly wigs, and lacy collars; of casting in the title role Fanny Salvini-Donatelli, who was considerably well-upholstered and no longer in her first youth; plus the poor singing of the rest of the cast, including Varesi, was bound to lead to disaster.

Back home Verdi found Giuseppina ill and depressed. She had read rumours in a magazine about a relationship between Verdi and a female singer. Giuseppina was not blind to his weaknesses, and she could see that money was a draw that made him 'work like a slave' in order to 'accumulate it',[81] but she loved him all the same, and put up with his occasional brusqueness, his irritability, and bad temper. She knew that he was 'stubborn as a mule', but he had the 'heart of an angel'.[82] 'We may have our youth behind us, but we still mean more to each other than all the world,' she had written to her 'magician' in Venice when she was 37.[83] They both spent September that year in Naples, in a house by the sea that his friend De Sanctis had arranged for them. It was supposed to be a *secret*, Verdi said, and he did not want *either to hear operas or suggestions for operas* while he was there.[84] The following month they both set off for Paris.

'At the Best Theatre in the World' · 1853–1860

Paris held a special attraction for Verdi, despite the many difficulties he had working with the Opéra (about which he never ceased to complain) and despite all his grumbles over wasted time, the cold and the fog. For the centre of the operatic world was here, not in Italy. Nowhere else did opera have such fascination for the general public. There was even one occasion on which the French parliament was unable to sit because so many of the deputies were at the première of Meyerbeer's *Le Prophète*. Parisians were held spellbound by the dazzling sets, the polished choreography, the seemingly infinite depth of the stage, the wonderfully life-like catastrophes, crowd scenes, and other stage spectacles, the lights and the colours, and by the magic of sophisticated dioramas – scenes painted on transparent backcloths and lit from behind to produce astonishing illusions. For the first time electric light was used in *Le prophète* to create a sunrise and, at the end, a huge fire, both of which left an unforgettable impression on the audience. Another reason why French Grand Opéra was so popular at this time was its topicality. Historical subjects, such as the Anabaptists in *Le prophète*, or the St Bartholomew's Day Massacre in *Les Huguenots* (1836), held up a mirror to contemporary concerns such as the continued independence of the social revolutionary movement, or the manipulation of the masses.

The most famous opera composer of his time, Meyerbeer was a source of great interest to Verdi. If he was to succeed in Paris he

L'Académie Royale de Musique, 1844. The name of the Opéra was changed after each political revolution. Ten years later it was known as the Théâtre Impérial de l'Opéra. This opera house, directed by Duponchel, had nearly 2,000 seats and was in production all year round.

would have to deal with a new set of problems. The greater scale of French Grand Opéra meant composing a historical piece in five acts complete with a long ballet. Apart from the musical subtlety of Meyerbeer's operas – which Berlioz used as examples of orchestration in his treatise on instrumentation – Verdi was most fascinated by the great chorus scenes and spectacular tableaux, in particular the benediction of the swords in *Les Huguenots* and the coronation in *Le prophète*. Here the competition was for originality, rather like that between piano and violin virtuosi, and the winner was the composer who could outdo previous effects and excite the audience with visual and musical novelties. Verdi would rather have resisted this tendency, as his own preference was for the most concise and simplest effects. He had an acute sense of the theatrical, but he made no concessions to his audience's taste for the macabre: the massacre at the end of his new opera *Les vêpres siciliennes* is glimpsed only for a brief moment, accompanied by a chorus of fanatical barbarians. Even Meyerbeer, at the première of *Les Huguenots*, had to admit that 'success in the madness of the present-day' was enough 'to make you blush', but he was also a consummate self-promoter and knew very well how to *bring the Press up to the boil six months before a success*, as Verdi noted, quoting from a newspaper.[85]

Verdi's contract with Roqueplan, the intendant, for an opera at the *best theatre in the world*[86] was signed in February 1852. It went without saying that the text would be written by Eugène Scribe (1791–1861), Meyerbeer's librettist and the most famous in Europe. In the libretto on which he and Verdi finally agreed (which had gathered a little dust, having been offered both to Halévy and Donizetti as *Le Duc d'Albe*), there was one major scene that Verdi immediately adopted for *Les vêpres siciliennes*: in it Montfort, the French Governor, is prepared to pardon the conspirators only if his son, Henri, one of their number, will address him as 'Father' – Henri finally acquiesces in order to save his beloved Hélène, and thereby prevents the execution at the very last moment. The drama inherent in this scene – the impending revolt, the preparations for the execution, the ruler who begs for his son's love in front of all the people, and finally the long-sought 'mon père' (my father) – made Verdi set aside any misgivings. Composing the opera, however, did not come

Premières at the Paris Grand Opéra:

1828   *La muette de Portici (The Dumb Girl of Portici*, also known as *Masaniello)* by Auber

1829   *Guillaume Tell (William Tell)* by Rossini

1831   *Robert le diable (Robert the Devil)* by Meyerbeer

1835   *La Juive (The Jew)* by Halévy

1836   *Les Huguenots* by Meyerbeer

1838   *Benvenuto Cellini* by Berlioz

1847   *Jérusalem* by Verdi

1849   *Le Prophète (The Prophet)* by Meyerbeer

1855   *Les vêpres siciliennes (The Sicilian Vespers)* by Verdi

1863   *Les Troyens (The Trojans)* by Berlioz

1865   *L'Africaine (The African)* by Meyerbeer

1867   *Don Carlos* by Verdi

easily this time. When the eccentric soprano Sophia Cruvelli simply disappeared to the Côte d'Azur during rehearsals, Verdi secretly hoped that he might at last have a reason to turn his back on the Opéra – but Cruvelli returned. He became extremely angry with his singers during rehearsals and complained to Crosnier, the new intendant, about Scribe, who had not delivered the changes he had requested for the fifth act. The unhappy composer even tried to wriggle out of the contract, so he was mightily relieved when the opera was finally finished.

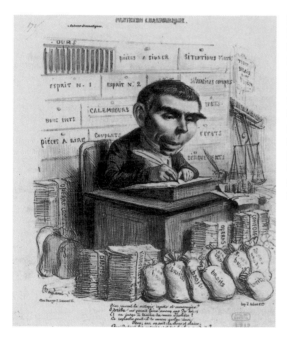

Librettist Eugène Scribe is caricatured as a merchant at his desk in his libretto factory. He is producing texts from spare parts filed in numerous drawers. Scribe only needs to add his signature (*pièces à signer*). The libretti are piled up around him, along with sacks containing the proceeds of copyright sales.

In *Les Vêpres siciliennes* Verdi had followed the conventions of French Grand Opéra almost to the letter. It was on a historical subject – the uprising in Sicily against foreign rule by the French of 1282 – and he had incorporated numerous ideas from Meyerbeer's operas such as tableaux and sudden shocks; and he had even picked

EUGÈNE SCRIBE

the brains of the Neapolitan De Sanctis about Sicilian folk dances so as to include a little local colour. In the finale of Act 2 Verdi combines the barcarole of the boat party with the chorus of enraged Sicilians, a contrast reminiscent of Act 3 of *Les Huguenots* where the Ave Maria ('Vierge Marie') is set contrapuntally against the rataplan of the soldiers. The duet between Hélène and Henri in Act 3 owes much to the famous duet in Act 4 of *Les Huguenots*, while Montfort's *Au sein de la puissance* is inspired melodically by the 'blessing of the swords'. Influenced by Meyerbeer's scores, Verdi had also chosen unusual sound effects, making expressive use of bass instruments. They did not go unnoticed, and Berlioz, writing in *La France musicale*, praised 'the rich variety of the instrumentation'.[88]

'Verdi is having to wrestle with all the Opéra people. Yesterday he made a terrible scene at the dress rehearsal. I feel sorry for the poor man.'

HECTOR BERLIOZ, to a friend, 1853[87]

Nevertheless, when all is said and done, Verdi had not written a Grand Opéra. In *Les vêpres siciliennes*, as in *Rigoletto*, it is above all the duets that stand out dramatically; not the great tableaux but the meetings between two characters who are closely bound to one another: two duets for the lovers, two for father and son. Henri, the vacillating hero with scruples; Montfort, the insecure and isolated governor; Hélène, initially intent on murdering the tyrant, but who forgets her grievances after she is pardoned – all these characters are uncertain of themselves, helplessly involved in a drama whose course is determined from the outset by the 'death' motif 𝄽 𝅘𝅥. 𝅘𝅥𝅮𝅘𝅥 𝄽, first heard on the timpani and drums in the overture. The only character who is not credible is Procida, the leader of the revolt. The revolutionaries in this opera also appear helpless, even incompetent, and therefore, after their abortive uprising, even their patriotic songs are untypical of grand opéra. The hymn to the fatherland (*O noble patrie*) is a sad song with hollow octaves and heavy accents, and even the spectacular orchestral accompaniment which follows cannot modify its hopelessness. There is no utopian vision of a different life to mitigate this catastrophe, no expectation of a 'waiting heaven' as in the death scenes of Verdi's earlier operas. It is the gentle melody of the muted first violins at the end of Act 4 that lingers in the memory, as they pick up Hélène's *Adieu mon pays, je succombe*, in a different rhythm, very slowly and, as in the overture, accompanied by the so-called 'death' figures – the grief of a farewell. The first performance had some success, despite the anti-French nature of the subject matter, but *Les vêpres siciliennes* never found a secure place in the repertory.

Verdi did not return to Sant'Agata until December 1855. He was exhausted and angry after disagreements with his publisher Tito Ricordi (the son of Giovanni) over carelessly handled negotiations and faulty editions. There were also disputes with Calzado, the impresario at the Théâtre Italien in Paris, over unpaid royalties. And Verdi was again suffering from mysterious stomach pains, as was usual after he had finished work on an opera. He wrote to Clara Maffei at the beginning of April: *I am doing nothing, no reading, no writing. I walk in the fields from morning to evening and try to recover . . . Cursed, cursed operas!*[89] The following summer in Paris he lost his legal case against Calzado to claim author's rights. A foreigner had no royalty rights, and could scarcely even defend himself against pirated editions – and this was also the case in England. Work on the French version of *Il trovatore*, which had its première at the Opéra as *Le trouvère* early in 1857, also took up his time. He was corresponding with Piave from Paris about a reworking of *Stiffelio*, but he was principally concerned with a new opera for Venice, persuaded into it by Piave once more. Like *Il trovatore*, it would be based on a play by the Spaniard Gutiérrez. The subject this time would be a fourteenth-century Doge (a chief magistrate), Simon Boccanegra.

Verdi was so impatient that he was apparently unwilling to correspond with Piave on the text. He blithely asked Giuseppe Montanelli – an author and lawyer from Tuscany living in exile in Paris – to rework Piave's manuscript. Then he sent Piave the finished libretto with the laconic comment *it was necessary* – he could put his name to it or not as he wished.[90] When Verdi felt himself to be in the wrong, he could be particularly blunt and hurtful, in this case with a friend whom he had previously defended against critics who considered Piave to be a dreadful librettist.

The new opera, *Simon Boccanegra*, was not well received by critics or the public. It was not just its dark orchestral colour, the slow tempi, or the absence of large choruses, nor the newfangled arrangement of parts where low voices – a baritone and two basses – predominated. Arrigo Boito (1842–1918), later to become Verdi's librettist, compared it to 'a wobbly table, where you can't see which is the faulty leg'. He exempted the prologue from this criticism, since he found it 'really beautiful and strong in its thorough-going darkness' and 'as dark and solid as a piece of basalt rock'.[91] The fiasco at the first performance in Venice on 12 March 1857 was followed by further failures, so that *Simon Boccanegra* disappeared from the repertory. Many years later, in 1881, Verdi revised it thoroughly to create the version we know today.

Meanwhile Verdi had bought more land and a large estate. He would spend entire days in the fields, sometimes hunting in the water-meadows or riding through the woods. He was worn out by the pressure of working to fixed deadlines – he had been *on a chain for too long*, as he remarked to Giuseppina.[92] At the end of September 1857 they both attended the première in Rimini of *Aroldo*. *Stiffelio*, the drama about a pastor, had been turned into a crusader opera that went down well with the audience. Most of the music of *Aroldo* is the same as *Stiffelio*, though Act 4 was newly composed and the libretto was new. Verdi had known Angelo Mariani (1821–73), one of the best conductors in Italy, for more than ten years, and the success of *Aroldo* marked the beginning of a close friendship.

Mariani, who was nine years younger, shared Verdi's political views and both men sported a Mazzini beard. Mariani was principal conductor of the opera and the municipal orchestra in Genoa, where he was held in high regard. A passionate musician, he was also a sympathetic and highly animated conversationalist. Verdi, now 44, enjoyed the younger man's vitality – and nicknamed him 'Napoliello' (little Napoleon). They shared the same interest in literature, both collected manuscripts, and both loved hunting. Mariani, however, remained sufficiently independent to conduct operas by Meyerbeer, and later by Wagner.

Apart from Mariani and Piave, Verdi's other close friends included the sculptor Luccardi and the journalist Opprandino Arrivabene in Rome, as well as the businessman De Sanctis in Naples. Verdi made friends easily, and with them he dropped his usual reserve, a product of scepticism and mistrust, so that his manner was warm and direct, although he could still be rude from time to time. He had no qualms about enlisting his friends' services in various ways. He was always giving Mariani jobs to do: to collect pictures for him; to bring rare seeds, tubers, or plants from nurseries in Genoa (once it was ten magnolias, each 1.5 metres tall, packed in straw); to exchange a gun for him, but he must try the new one several times; then he needed seven iron railings for the large windows at Sant'Agata, which of course must first be

Angelo Mariani in 1857.

located, and they might be cheaper in Cremona than in Genoa. Mariani loyally carried out all Verdi's commissions; he brought things through customs (often paying for them himself), and he even found jobs for Verdi's protégés.

Hunting, playing cards, *boccia* or billiards, keeping pets – dogs, cats, fish, and various species of birds – were just some of the ways in which Verdi made up for the games he never played in childhood. He had a mischievous side, sending messages in the name of Loulou, his little Maltese dog, or posting letters to Arrivabene's Dobermann. In his daily concerns, however, he had little patience with letter-writing. He left the job of answering overdue correspondence to Giuseppina, whose elegant and witty way with words was far better than his *gruff style*, or so he said.[93] When he did pick up a pen he wrote spontaneously and without much care, with no pretensions to elegance, using numerous exclamation marks, and signing off at speed with a brief *Addio! Addio!*

In September 1857 Verdi once again returned to his pet project, *King Lear*, to fulfil his contract from the previous year with the Teatro San Carlo in Naples. This tragedy of a king and father made to suffer by his children was a subject that seems almost to have obsessed Verdi, from *Oberto* to *Aida*. He had already worked with Cammarano on a libretto for *Re Lear* (*King Lear*), and had even sketched out a scenario in four acts. Even after Cammarano's unexpected death he had not abandoned his plan to compose this opera in a *completely new manner, without regard for conventions.*[94] He had been corresponding since the spring of 1853 with Antonio Somma about *Re Lear*, although he sometimes despaired at the difficulty of reducing such a huge and complex tragedy to an opera libretto. Somma, a lawyer, journalist and author, had been for many years the director of the Teatro Grande in Trieste. Verdi admired his abilities and was always polite when he wrote to him. The composer took notice when Somma raised objections, but he nevertheless insisted on his point of view, so the manuscript was rewritten many times.

Unlike Wagner, who always felt the need to explain himself and his art, Verdi shied away from self-explanation. It was rare for him to write about his artistic aims or his aesthetic principles in his letters, but on the few occasions when he did, it was almost always to Somma. For Verdi the *effetto* (effectiveness on the stage) was at the heart of his decisions. *Varietà* – the principle of variety and change which he found particularly evident in Shakespeare's plays – was also vital to keep the interest of the audience. For Verdi, monotony was the greatest sin, so he was continually urging his librettists to brevity and precision. He complained to Piave about *lines that are partially or completely superfluous, makeweights – 'Ah!s, 'Eh!s and 'Oh!s – which are just there to pad out the syllables.*[95] Theatre required the *parola scenica* – writing that is effective on the stage and immediately characterises a given situation. *I know very well*, he wrote to Somma, *that 'Prepare yourself for death', or 'Commend your soul to the Lord' mean the same thing, but on stage they do not have the same power as the simple 'You must die!'*[96] He took an interest in – and gave great importance to – nuances within the Italian language. He found the rhythm of some lines too harsh and asked Somma to change certain rhymes – such as *è dessi/adesso* – and he reminded the librettist how dangerous it was to use proverbs or figures of speech on the operatic stage.

Whether or not *Re Lear* could be mounted on the stage depended to a large extent on the singers available to the company. For this opera it would not be sufficient to have just two or three good soloists – there were at least five main roles. And where would they find a baritone who could play Lear? Singers were not trained to present character. A dearth of suitable talent meant that *Re Lear* was postponed each season while other operas were written and performed, until finally, after more than 15 years, Verdi abandoned the project.

After searching long and hard, he chose a play by Scribe for his last contract with the San Carlo in Naples. Its subject was the murder of Gustav III, King of Sweden, at a masked ball in 1792, and it had already been made into an opera by Auber (*Gustave III ou Le bal masqué*, 1833). Verdi shortened Scribe's play by more than a third and had Somma put it into verse. The assassination of a head of State was a risky subject, especially in reactionary Naples, so Somma wrote under a pseudonym. At the very last minute, when Somma had almost finished, the theatre informed Verdi that the censor had refused to pass the libretto, despite new names and locations for the action and a change of title from *Gustavo III di Svezia* to *Una vendetta in Domino*. The censor stipulated that the action must take place outside Europe, preferably in the Middle Ages. Furthermore, the lovers must under no circumstances be married and a murder on stage was completely out of the question. The scene in which lots are drawn had to be omitted and the whole ball scene was suspect. As ever, Verdi was unwilling to contemplate such drastic changes and the theatre claimed 5,000 ducats from him in compensation. The composer avoided having to pay by submitting a counter-claim. In place of *Una vendetta in Domino* the San Carlo took *Simon Boccanegra*. On the advice of his friend Luccardi, Verdi then offered *Una vendetta* to the Apollo Theatre in Rome, but although the situation there was less repressive than in Naples, the papal censors listed a whole series of lines where Somma had to make changes yet again. The action was moved to the politically acceptable city of Boston, the Swedish king became a British governor, and the title became *Un ballo in maschera* (*A Masked Ball*).

Time and place are not of crucial importance in this opera, since politics is not its main subject. Here the conspirators have personal rather than political motives for their actions; the death of the governor is merely the result of an error and at the end the

In this 1858 caricature Vincenzo Torelli, Secretary at the Teatro San Carlo, looks displeased as he studies the objections of the censors to Somma's libretto for *Un ballo in maschera*.

conspirators even join the chorus in a prayer, to harp accompaniment. The opera does, however, express a feeling prevalent in Verdi's time: the loss of political ideals, and the isolation of the individual adrift in a faceless society.

The community seek diversion in dancing a wild galop, in which their masks indicate that socialising can only take place anonymously. But all these glittering trappings – of which the page, Oscar, sings with such naive joy – are merely a front behind which lurks something far more menacing. It is for this reason that the dance music and the ever-present conspirators' motif are heard simultaneously. The revenge trio in Act 3 (*Dunque l'onta*), points up just how much of an empty pose revolution – the fighting spirit of the Risorgimento – has become. Here the voices adopt in unison the rhythm of the *Ernani* chorus *Si ridesti il Leon di Castiglia*,

♪.♪|♩ ♪.♪♩ ♫♫ |♩. ♪♪, the appeal to arms against the oppressors, which is now an ironic reference. In the oath scene, too, with its brass and tremolo strings, the conspirators, whose rather vague motives have barely been touched upon in Act 3, appear to be play-acting. They are denoted by a staccato motif quite devoid of passion and fire. In Act 2 they comment on the misfortunes of others *derisively*, in a slow and sensuous tempo. They represent a society for which tragedy has become merely a laughing matter. Ulrica's scene makes the fear and menace tangible, as if truth in a world of deception and error has retreated to the gypsies' encampment. The alternations in this scene between comedy and terror, between charlatans and those in deadly earnest, between cries of 'Viva!' and sentences of death, all point up the ambivalence between tragedy and comedy that is the hallmark of this opera.

The three protagonists are presented in a more precise fashion than hitherto, with an emphasis on their psychological traits. Neither the close bonds of marriage nor friendship can protect them from treachery and betrayal. A best friend can turn into a murderer if he believes himself deceived. Society is an illusion, and even the bonds of the family are no protection. Amelia, unhappily married, goes in search of a *herb* to protect her from her true feelings, but instead encounters the spectres of her fear and servitude. The introductory chorus suggests that Riccardo is inhabiting a *beautiful dream*. A type of lullaby, it is comic as a homage to a governor, and it soon clashes grotesquely with the conspirators' motif, which is heard at the same time. Riccardo accepts this ambiguous homage of the people in a light-hearted manner, quite unlike a political leader, while the people are confident their *well-being* is *at the centre of his thoughts*, which, in fact, are all with Amelia. His first council meeting is accompanied by a playful tune with mocking trills. Ever on the lookout for distraction, he hatches a bold plan to visit the gypsy fortune-teller in disguise. The breathtaking tempo of his

In these caricatures Verdi, Fraschini, Fioretti, and the dog Loulou rehearse *Un ballo in maschera*.

reckless *Allegro brillante* is reminiscent of Don Giovanni's champagne aria. However, Riccardo's mood swings, his irresponsibility, and his forced jollity are all indicative of a melancholy, even suicidal man. His unrequited love for Amelia, around which his thoughts and feelings constantly revolve, is characterised by a repeated tune, full of longing, with its accent on the seventh in F sharp major. It is this key that denotes remoteness and dreams, here with inflections towards the minor mode. The barcarole, which Riccardo sings dressed as a fisherman, belongs with the part he is playing, but it also betrays his longing for a different life in its range of melody, hovering between major and minor. Breathless impatience can be heard in the chromatic staccato phrase, while a frivolous glissando before *la morte* reveals that his joie de vivre is in reality a longing for death. Finally Riccardo introduces, with a laugh, the subsequent concertato with its intimation of his approaching death (*È scherzo od è follia*).

The lovers' duet, when they meet and confront their inner selves, is the central point of *Un ballo in maschera*, when they finally live in the present. As the music reveals, it is the unfeigned expression of desire, both utterly sensual and at the same time filled with an insatiable longing for which there is no place in the real world. Their meeting-place, beneath the gallows, is a stark visual reminder of this fact. Riccardo's belief in the possibility of a life lived in harmony with the world, a vision he clings to as he dies (explaining the murder and pardoning, even thanking, everyone) is suddenly and brutally snuffed out by his death.

The unexpected and spectacular popular success of the first performance of *Un ballo in maschera* in Rome on 17 February 1859 did not change Verdi's attitude to the theatre. He was thoroughly tired of it, especially as the production was actually rather bad and the reviews were critical. He wanted finally to leave his *galley years* behind him with *Un ballo in maschera*. He was 45 and this was his twenty-first opera.[97]

On their way home from Rome, Verdi and Giuseppina could not help but notice the preparations for war: soldiers had been recruited in Turin; billeting and requisitions led to Austria demanding in an ultimatum that the number of troops in Piedmont be reduced.

In 1859 Francis Joseph of Austria and Napoleon III signed the Treaty of Villafranca. Lombardy was ceded and an Italian Confederation was to be formed. The puppet rulers of Parma, Modena and Tuscany, were to be reinstated. Cavour regarded this as a total defeat, as it left Austria still a member of the Italian Confederation.

Verdi and Giuseppina had been at home a mere ten days when, on 31 March 1859, Austria declared war on Piedmont – they could hear the thunder of the cannon almost every day in Sant'Agata. After the army of Napoleon III came to Piedmont's aid in mid-May, the Austrians were defeated on 24 June at the Battle of Solferino. However, after all the sacrifices they had made, the Italians were shocked by the terms of the Treaty of Villafranca and considered it a betrayal by Napoleon III: Austria still held Venetia, Tuscany, and Modena. Lombardy was now given to France. In 1860, Lombardy received the new state of Sardinia-Piedmont from France, but had to cede Savoy and Nice in its place. Verdi had no wish to compose a hymn for Napoleon III, so instead he set up a fund for the victims of the war and made a personal donation of 550 francs.

It was probably while the war was being fought that Giuseppe Fortunino Francesco Verdi and Giuseppina Clelia Maria Josepha Strepponi decided to marry in the autumn of 1859 in the remote town of Collonges-sous-Salève. They were both in their mid-forties. It seems almost beyond comprehension that Verdi should have hesitated for so long, while Giuseppina had wanted to be married for many years. We do at least know how astonished people were in Milan when they discovered that she had been known as 'Madame Verdi' in Paris since 1854, for the Countess Appiani, a longtime friend of Verdi's, used it as a reason to distance herself from the couple.

Garibaldi in Naples. Verdi wrote to Clara Maffei: *Where is the promised independence for Italy for which we have hoped so long? . . . So much blood for nothing! So many poor disappointed young people!*[98]

Most theatres remained closed during the winter of 1859. Unemployment, scarce resources, and new disturbances were all consequences of the war. Piave had lost his position in Venice, and it was only after Verdi intervened that he was given the post of stage director at La Scala – where circumstances were also rather dire. Muzio fared rather better. Like his teacher Verdi, he might have languished in Busseto, but was now concert master at the Theatre Royal in London, and the following year acquired fame and fortune as a conductor in the United States. Most of the Italian states joined Sardinia-Piedmont following a plebiscite in 1860, and Verdi became Busseto's representative in the provincial assembly. He was one of five people deputed to inform Victor Emmanuel II of the people's vote. Shortly after this he made the personal acquaintance of Cavour, who determined policy for the new state the following year as head of the Turin Parliament. Meeting Cavour made a great impression on Verdi. At Cavour's request, he stood for election as a Deputy in the spring of 1860, though he was realistic enough to know that they were using his name and popularity to confer additional prestige on the new state. The great gulf between the majority of the population and the ruling class was shown by the fact that more than half were illiterate and only two per cent of the population were entitled to vote. This casts some doubt on the tradition that the name of Verdi was popularly read as an acronym for Victor Emmanuel Re d'Italia: a political motto for the proclamation of Victor Emmanuel II as King of Italy. It is a myth that links the name of Verdi for ever with the Italian nation state. Verdi himself understood little about the business of politics and took his lead

The *Académie Française* is the oldest of the five bodies that were incorporated into the the *Institut Français* in 1795. Its origin was in illegal weekly meetings that begin in 1630 in the house of Valentin Conrat, before being given 'letters patent' by Cardinal Richelieu. The *Académie* formulated its rules, chief of which is 'to labour with all care and diligence to give certain rules to the language, to render it pure, eloquent, and capable of treating the arts and sciences.' This 'labour' continues to the present day.

mostly from Cavour, whose death in the summer of 1861 depressed him greatly. He gave up his seat in 1865.

Verdi was no longer composing, nor was he reading or listening to music, and he no longer played the piano. He had lived most of his life under the constant pressure of deadlines, making inconvenient journeys, rehearsing in often inadequate circumstances, arguing with singers, impresarios, and journalists, battling for his author's rights and against the decisions of the censors. Now he enjoyed his daily routine, particularly redesigning his house. When he was named an honorary member of the Académie Française he commented ironically that from now on he would belong to the *wigs*[99] He rose at 5 am to hunt quail; he oversaw the building works; he wrote letters after lunch and a short rest; he regularly went for a walk in the evening and retired to bed early. It seemed to him unlikely that he would ever return to the business of writing operas.

I was absent from the Chamber for more than two years, and have only attended very seldom since then. I have been tempted many times to tender my resignation but . . . I am still a deputy, entirely against my will and my inclinations. I am completely unsuited to this position, nor do I have the patience which is so necessary in this field . . . The 450 deputies are in fact only 449, since Verdi the deputy does not exist. Verdi to Piave on 8 February 1865.[100]

Opposition in His Own
Country · 1860–1869

Among the many offers Verdi received to compose another opera there was one that caught his eye in December 1860. This had been negotiated by the tenor Enrico Tamberlick (1820–89) who was engaged at the Imperial Theatre in St Petersburg. Verdi had composed nothing new for four years, but he accepted this contract, partly persuaded by Giuseppina, and partly because he had considerable expenses to cover for the redesign of his house. The censor in St Petersburg would not countenance an opera based on Victor Hugo's novel *Ruy Blas* (1838), in which a lackey triumphs over a nobleman, so Verdi decided instead on *Don Álvaro o la fuerza del sino* (1835), a play by Ángel Saavedra (1791–1865), who did much to establish Romanticism in Spain. As usual, Verdi worked at great speed, and in November he and Giuseppina set off on the long journey to Russia, accompanied by two servants and an interpreter. They took the precaution of ordering supplies of pasta, Bordeaux wine and champagne. By now they were used to travelling in comfort, taking suites in hotels and using the services of staff on the way. Verdi's annual income at this time has been estimated at 80,000 lire.[101]

Although the first performance of Verdi's new opera, *La forza del destino*, had to be postponed to the following year owing to the illness of the prima donna, he and Giuseppina stayed in Russia for three months. The première of *La forza del destino* finally took place at St Petersburg's Imperial Theatre the following year, on 10

November 1862. Italian operas were extremely popular in Russia, despite the best attempts of nationalists to promote Russian music – in particular the five Russian composers known as the 'Mighty Handful' (*Moguchaya kuchka*): Mili Balakirev (1836–1910), Alexander Borodin (1833–87), César Cui (1835–1918), Modest Mussorgsky (1839–81), and Nikolay Rimsky-Korsakov (1844–1908). Despite its gloomy plot, the first performance of Verdi's opera was a great success. This was due in large part to the lavish production and to the fact that St Petersburg was able to afford the high fees necessary to engage outstanding singers such as Caroline Barbot and Enrico Tamberlick. The tsar, who received the composer in his box, decorated Verdi with the Order of Stanislaus.

Verdi in Russia, c.1861. *I have a magnificent apartment, kept at a spring temperature of 13 or 14 degrees, and two horses that run like the wind.*[102]

La forza del destino opens with the destruction of a family idyll, setting the three protagonists on an unalterable course. The story reveals a stark contrast between a life imbued with class arrogance, racial hatred, and revenge, and an unattainable longing for peace.

MIGHTY HANDFUL

The 'Mighty Handful'. By the 19th century Western influences of polyphony and harmony were making an impression on Russian music. On the estates of the aristocracy music based on Italian and Austrian models found an enthusiastic reception. Western musical influences had also been introduced into the imperial chapel.

Mikhail Glinka (1804–1857) was the first composer to fuse these musical traditions. His *Life for the Tsar* is generally regarded as the first Russian opera, performed in St Petersburg in 1836. Glinka used a Russian theme and folk melodies in an Italian-style format.

Mili Balakirev (1836–1910) became the acknowledged leader of this school of composers concerned to create a distinctively Russian style of music. They included Alexander Borodin, César Cui, Modest Mussorgsky and Nikolay Rimsky-Korsakov. The critic Vladimir Stasov, the moving spirit behind the group, called them *moguchaya kuchka* the 'Mighty Handful'. Mussorgsky's orchestration and harmonies, considered unplayable at first, belied his remarkable talent. Of the 'handful', it is his and Rimsky-Korsakov's influence on future generations of musicians that proved the most long-lived.

The force that compels the characters to act, isolating them and setting them against each other, has its basis in social conditions and the stark code of honour of the Spanish aristocracy under which Carlo exacts his revenge. This necessity (for which the term 'fate' is merely a metaphor) is given musical expression by a repeated motif for the wind – three long notes, reminiscent of the curse motifs in *Ernani* and *Rigoletto* – with which both the overture and the first two acts open. The feelings of fear and hopelessness engendered by this force can be heard in an orchestral theme

running through all four acts and almost continuously in the overture. This theme, with its agitated rhythm, turns within a narrow range around the same note, while the arching lines of Leonora's melody (a theme also repeated elsewhere) demonstrate the hope

Alvaro
1.Akt, 3.Szene

cantabile *dolcissimo*

ma d'a - mor si - - pu - ro e san - to

of another world. The concept of reconciliation is shown in the cantilena for Alvaro, the exotic stranger. The religious tone of this longing for utopia does not, however, obscure the equivocal role of the Church in the world. The individual does not know himself – as is shown in the many disguises and false names – and he is unable to make close contact with others. Verdi changed the dark ending of the opera – Alvaro's suicide – for the version to be performed in Milan in 1869. After the tragedy had reached its lowest point, marked by the orchestra with the harsh, dreadful 'death' figures, Verdi added a final trio of reconciliation in the dying Leonora's vision of a better future in the 'promised land'.

Neither the lavish choral scenes with their somewhat gaudy, stock-in-trade elements of the picturesque inn or the military camp, nor the comedy of Trabuco and Melitone, appear to present the life of the ordinary people as one of suffering, yet they nevertheless act as a cynical commentary on the dramatic events. The social contradictions of the period in which this opera was written are evident once again in the juxtaposition of enthusiasm for the war (the effective rataplan chorus), the pilgrims' prayers, the feeding of the poor, and the begging victims of war. However, *La forza del destino* was not successful in blending together different styles, in integrating its individual images into an underlying theme, or in achieving the synthesis of tragedy and comedy, all of which were so successfully realised in *Un ballo in maschera*.

One month after his fiftieth birthday Verdi read in a journal an article that both angered and hurt him. The librettist Arrigo Boito had written a strongly worded 'Ode to Italian Art' for the première of an opera by the young composer Franco Faccio (1840–91) in which he argued that the 'altar of art had been sullied' like a 'brothel' by the officially accepted music and literature of the day.[103] Verdi could not get over this insult and quoted the phrase repeatedly in his letters.

Viewed for a while as tone-setters in Clara Maffei's salon, Boito and Faccio were the spokesmen for a group of young musicians, writers, and journalists known as the La Scapigliatura ('the Bohemians'). This late-Romantic avant-garde accused the Catholic Church, the novelist Alessandro Manzoni, and Italian opera in general of being embedded in 'formulas' but lacking in 'form'. Their criticism was levelled at the works of Rossini, Donizetti, Bellini, and Verdi. Although he mocked the pretentious language of La Scapigliatura in his letters to Piave, Verdi was more cautious in his judgement of Boito and Faccio when communicating with Clara Maffei. These young men made him feel his age, but he maintained a reserved politeness towards them, pretending to be indifferent, even stating that he understood nothing of musical aesthetics and that he never read the scores of other composers. The music that he ordered from his publisher did nevertheless include many contemporary compositions. Faccio's first opera was unable to hold its own on the stage, but the next one – Amleto, with a libretto by Boito based on Shakespeare's Hamlet – was regarded as very promising. In contrast, after the première of his newly revised Macbeth, Verdi was told that he did not understand Shakespeare.

In the spring of 1865 the highly regarded music critic Filippi (who also belonged to La Scapigliatura) published an article stating

La Scapigliatura was a group of Romantic writers and artists who adopted a bohemian lifestyle in Milan between 1860 and 1880. They rebelled against bourgeois traditions in art and morality in favour of a greater immediacy and originality. The name derives from a novel by one of the group, La Scapigliatura e il 6 febbraio (1862) by Carlo Righetti.

that the 'Italian school' had been surpassed. It is clear how popular Meyerbeer's operas were in Italy at that time as they were the first to be published in the new pocket scores. Interest in German music, particularly instrumental, works, was also growing as is shown by the foundation of a Quartet Society in Milan in 1862. The supporters of the avant-garde gradually became adherents of Wagner. The journal *L'arpa*, published by Lucca, offered them a forum, whereas the Ricordi publishing house (Verdi's publisher) represented the more conservative and traditional, despite the fact that the young Giulio Ricordi, the son of Tito, was a supporter of La Scapigliatura.

At this time Verdi had heard only the overture to Wagner's *Tannhäuser* (1843–5, rev 1861–75), and had subsequently written to Arrivabene: 'He is mad!!!'[104] Verdi found the imputation that he himself was attempting to imitate Wagner or Meyerbeer quite intolerable, whereas he had aimed through his own music to raise the profile of Italy in the world. After reading Bizet's critical review of the first performance of *Don Carlos* (1867) – in which the Frenchman wrote 'Verdi is no longer an Italian. He follows Wagner'[105] – Verdi tried not to let his bitterness show, accepting the criticism in a laconic manner and even pretending to Opprandino Arrivabene that he did not care about the fate of his operas nearly so much as he did about his building work at the Villa Sant'Agata.

The Italian Minister for Education apparently agreed with La Scapigliatura when he complained that no Italian since Rossini had composed anything of note. In order to reinvigorate and reform Italian music he appointed Rossini president of a state music committee. In the summer of 1868, when Verdi was to be presented with the Commander of the Order of the Italian Crown, the composer deliberately provoked a scandal by letting it be known publicly that he would accept no honour from a minister *who had*

Verdi in 1870. Tall, thin, but robust looking is how his contemporaries described him. 'Two deep creases in his cheeks, sharp features, heavy eyebrows, restless eyes, large mouth, bitter and disdainful.'[106]

pronounced so heavy a sentence on an art which bore the name of Italy aloft with honour throughout the world.[107]

When Angelo Mariani visited in the spring of 1864 he found the newly remodelled Villa Sant'Agata had become a paradise. Verdi had even built on a little chapel in order to spare Giuseppina the long walk to church. They had brought back pictures and sculptures from their travels, and several rare plants for the garden – and from Paris an Érard grand piano. The rooms were decorated in upper-middle-class style, with heavy furniture, lavish curtains and hangings, and numerous paintings, vases, and figurines. Apart from Mariani and Piave there were often other guests including Ricordi, Clara Maffei, Luccardi, Arrivabene and Léon Escudier, Verdi's French publisher.

However, Verdi was not entirely free from disruption at Sant'Agata. In the summer of 1865 the citizens of Busseto violently disagreed on the subject of an opera house, which had been under construction since 1861, and was to bear Verdi's name. Verdi himself thought a theatre entirely unnecessary, particularly given the exigencies of the current economic situation. Naturally many people involved in the venture had hoped for a financial contribution from the wealthy composer. Verdi found it humiliating that indirect pressure was being applied on him to symbolically repay his student scholarship to study in Milan. Some people even considered themselves responsible for making him the man he was today. He made a bitter list of all the unpleasantnesses and injustices, large and small, that he had suffered in Busseto: the refusal of his own application (and the denial of Muzio's) for the position of music master; the constant malicious gossip; the opposition to his irrigation project; various disputes with the local authority; and the snubbing of Giuseppina over many years. In the end the theatre was named after Verdi, who gave 10,000 lire towards it; but he never went inside. When it was inaugurated in 1868 with *Rigoletto*, Verdi and his wife were taking the waters in Tabiano.

In the winter Mariani had rented two floors of the Palazzo Sauli for the Verdis. It was a villa surrounded by a large garden on the Carignano hills in Genoa where they spent the winter months for seven years from 1866 onwards. Mariani lived in the apartment next to theirs and arranged furniture, carpets, and curtains for their rooms so that everything was perfectly organised when they moved in. Verdi felt happy in this beautiful house, the mild air

Verdi's luxurious winter quarters on the first floor of the Palazzo Sauli in Genoa, which contained reception rooms, guest rooms, and servants' quarters.

did him good, and Mariani's company was stimulating after the isolation of Sant'Agata.

At the end of August 1865, Arrivabene was pleased to detect hints about a new opera in one of Verdi's joking letters written in the name of his dog. *Mad* as he was, Verdi was considering *making a few more scrawls.*[108] He was referring to the fact that he might accept an offer from Perrin to compose a new work for the Opéra. Visiting Sant'Agata the previous summer, Escudier had proposed Schiller's *Don Carlos* (1787) and Joseph Méry and Camille du Locle were to make a French libretto from the play. In November 1865 Verdi and his wife went to Paris. They stayed over three months and, in their apartment on the Champs Élysées, regularly entertained guests, including Rossini and his wife; Escudier; Du Locle; the tenors Fraschini and Tamberlick; the sculptor Dantan; and the famous singer Adelina Patti. They also took part in the 'musical Saturdays' at Rossini's salon.

In June 1866 Verdi was back home in Sant'Agata, hard at work on *Don Carlos* when war broke out between Austria and Prussia. Italy was drawn into the fighting after a promise was made to cede the Venetio to Italy should Austria be defeated. While Boito, Faccio, and Giulio Ricordi were all fighting with Garibaldi's troops, Verdi was almost ashamed to be bound by his contract with the Paris Opéra. Sant'Agata lay near the front line, so the Verdis had to be prepared for enemy troops to cross the Po. After the Prussian victory on 3 July at Königgrätz, Italy was once again ignored by the Great Powers, who first handed Venice to Napoleon III of France. He then ceded it to Italy. This was seen as a humiliation by the Italian people. Thoroughly disillusioned, Verdi tried in vain to cancel his contract with the Opéra, but in September he had to be in Paris once more to supervise rehearsals that would continue for six months.

A journalist who observed Verdi during rehearsals of *Don Carlos* recorded his impressions in

In June 1866, Prussia proposed that the Frankfurt *Bundestag* be abolished and a *Bund* established. Austria mobilised nine German states in opposition, and war began on 14 June. On 3 July, at Königgratz, or Sadowa, on the Elbe, north east of Prague, the Austrian army was crushed by the Prussians.

Le Figaro: Verdi sat opposite the conductor, pale-faced and as 'motionless as an Assyrian god', but with 'burning eyes'. The composer's extraordinary hearing missed nothing. Occasionally he jumped to his feet, called out, marked the beat, or ran on to the stage.[109]

Verdi's last work for the Paris Opéra and also his last to be based on a play by Schiller, *Don Carlos* was something of a gamble. Ten years after the disaster with *Les vêpres siciliennes* he had again accepted the challenge of grand opéra; thereby inviting comparison not only with Meyerbeer, but also with the composers of the Théâtre Lyrique such as Ambroise Thomas (1811–96), whose greatest success was *Mignon* (1866), and Charles Gounod (1818–93), composer of *Faust* (1859), and last but not least with Wagner, whose *Tristan und Isolde* had had its première in Munich in 1865.

Verdi was unwilling, as with his earlier Schiller settings, to reduce Schiller's drama to emotional conflicts, to neglect the intellectual issues involved, or to reduce the historical background – absolutism under Philip II of Spain; the fanaticism of the Inquisition; the war of liberation in the Netherlands – to mere background colour. He also insisted on including the discussions between Philippe (the king), Posa, and the Grand Inquisitor in the libretto. As a result *Don Carlos* is Verdi's longest opera. He was obliged to make cuts in the music during rehearsals so that the audience could catch their last trains back to the suburbs after the performance. What is more, Verdi worked on the opera during the next decade and more, making three different versions. The Italian version of 1882–3 for La Scala is the best known; it is shortened to four acts, omitting the Fontainebleau act and the ballet. A five-act Italian version was performed in Modena in 1886, but it is only in our own time that the French five-act version has been staged again.

This version opens in Fontainebleau, the one place in the opera not surrounded by palace walls or under the watchful eye of the Inquisition. The first meeting between Carlos and Elisabeth is like a fairy-tale, with the princess lost in the forest, distributing gifts like the legendary saint. It is therefore not passion but an innocent, almost fairy-tale love that is expressed in Carlos's C major romance. Then, after their ecstatic love duet in D-flat major, the

dream is rudely shattered. Political realities demand that Elisabeth marry the king, Philippe, and her happiness at Fontainebleau remains as a memory, encapsulated in the themes of the romance and the duet, which return later in the opera. The subsequent four acts present the conflict between father and son, and the tragedy of the powerless monarch, the suffering he feels at the impossibility of combining private happiness and public position – all achieved more clearly and forcefully than in any of the earlier operas. An awareness of social collapse (which so imbued Verdi's own period) is shown in the disintegration of the family and the gulf between private and public life. Philippe's isolation is clearly demonstrated by the fact that the eight duets in the opera include not a single one for father and son, or for Philippe and Elisabeth.

Philippe's night-time monologue in the fourth act reflects the melancholy consciousness of modern man, aware he has been relegated to a cold and solitary existence. His initial thoughts return at the end to their point of departure, but it is not just the construction of the monologue that reveals how all his thoughts are dominated by the hopelessness of his pain. Three long notes – reminiscent of the 'fate' or 'curse' motifs in other Verdi operas – reinforce the impression of the inescapable. It is the persistent circularity of the orchestral motifs in particular, with neither beginning nor end, which point up his endless musings. Although a strong desire for life is asserted in the B major section, following the andante in D minor, the return to the despair of the opening is depressing nevertheless. The subtle transition in the aria from a declamatory opening to an arioso, the variation in the instrumentation, and particularly the solo cello line resembling the human voice to reveal inner feelings, all reminded many listeners of Wagner, although Verdi had tried many of these effects before in *Macbeth*. In addition, the dark melody in bare octaves that accompanies the dialogue between Philippe and the Grand Inquisitor is remarkably similar to the theme of the strings during Rigoletto's first meeting with Sparafucile; although the impression of inevitability in Don Carlos is made more debilitating and threatening by its extremely low register, the minor key, and the dark sound of the contra-bassoon.

There had been a growing concentration on scenes of grieving and farewell in Verdi's operas since the 1850s, but in *Don Carlos* he also expressed his scepticism about the political stagnation in Italy. Posa's views on freedom are clearer than they are in Schiller's play. Here his dream of the *dawning* of a peaceful world concludes in Philippe's warning against the Grand Inquisitor, while his vision of the *salvation of Spain* as he lies dying is marred by the imprisoning of the Infanta which immediately follows. Again, a short while later, hope is shown to be completely misplaced for the general populace as they beg forgiveness for their brief revolt, frightened by the mere appearance of the Grand Inquisitor. The idea of brotherly love in this period of inequality remains merely a fine concept for which to hope. This is given musical expression as Carlos and Posa swear an oath of friendship in their duet, a brilliant hymn in C major with a march rhythm. The voices, singing in parallel, ring out like a fanfare and might well waken the 'sweet notions of equality' about which Schiller's Don Carlos dreams (Act I, Scene 9, line 1006). Yet when Posa disarms his friend in the finale of Act 3, by taking his sword, two lone clarinets introduce the motif of friendship, with almost no bass, and they do not play it in full. In Act 4 a sad motif on the cornet accompanied by 'death' figures on the drums remind the listener of Carlos's and Posa's hymn, before it is heard one last time, played quietly and a third lower, to accompany Posa's dying words.

How the many contrasting scenes of this 'grand opera' form a single unity – to constitute, in Verdi's words, *a work poured from one mould* rather than a *mosaic*[110] – is a question that does not seem to have been fully resolved, even in *Don Carlos* with its great through-composed scenes and recurring motifs. The many changes Verdi later made were all attempts to combine the spectacular stage effects (the *auto-da-fé* or the popular revolt) with the subtle characterisations of ennui, dreams of liberation, and elegant diversions (the veil song and the 15-minute ballet) into a single musical drama. Opinions on *Don Carlos* were divided. The première was only a moderate success.

1867 was an unhappy year. In January, while Verdi was in Paris preparing for the first performance of *Don Carlos*, his father died. Verdi was unable to attend his funeral. Carlo Verdi and his sister had been bringing up a granddaughter, seven-year-old Filomena, and now Verdi and Giuseppina became her guardians. Giuseppina's son, Camillo, had died five years previously, although there is no reference to his death in her letters or diaries. The Verdis were fond of Filomena and it upset them to be parted from her; nevertheless they sent her to a good boarding school in Turin.

More bad news followed. Piave had a stroke at the end of the year and was left disabled and unable to speak for the rest of his life. Verdi supported Piave's family financially, and he also visited his old friend whenever he was in Milan. At Verdi's instigation an album of songs by well-known Italian composers was put together for Piave's benefit. Next, the death of the 80-year-old Antonio Barezzi plunged Verdi into deep mourning. *You know that I owe him everything, everything,* he wrote to Clara Maffei. *I loved him like my own father.*[111]

Giuseppina returned from a visit to Clara Maffei in Milan with an invitation from Alessandro Manzoni. So Verdi returned to Milan for the first time in 20 years, and his meeting with the 83-year-old author moved him deeply. His respect for men like Manzoni or Cavour was so great as to be almost childlike. *I would have gone down on my knees before him, if one could worship men,* he confessed to Clara Maffei.[112] He met his old friends again in her salon, and they were able to persuade him to allow his operas to be performed at La Scala once more.

When Rossini died in November 1868 Verdi decided to write a memorial for him and for Italian music. Twelve Italian composers were each to write one movement of a Requiem to be performed in Bologna on the first anniversary of Rossini's death; Bologna, Verdi insisted, being Rossini's *true home*.[113] He set the *Libera me*, but there was little enthusiasm for the project among the modernists, although younger composers were not invited to take part. In the end the tribute to Rossini failed mainly because of the tight deadline. The chorus and orchestra of the Bologna theatre were worn out after an exhausting schedule of operas, and Mariani, who was to conduct the Mass, was busy with another memorial for Rossini in Pesaro. Verdi, however, held Mariani wholly responsible for the failure of his plan and vented all his anger on him. Although Mariani had conducted Wagner's *Lohengrin* (1846–8) and *Die Meistersinger von Nürnberg* (*The Mastersingers of Nuremberg*, 1862–7) – for which he was not forgiven in Sant'Agata – he had played a major part in Verdi's success in Italy. Nevertheless, despite this unjust attack he remained loyal to Verdi. Verdi took it as a personal affront that *the national celebration* for which *the artistic community of the whole of Italy* should have been united, should find almost no support.[114] He was so disillusioned by the whole episode that he even tried to force Mariani, who was by then seriously ill with cancer, to clear out his apartment in the Palazzo Strozzi, purely so that they would never have to meet again.

'No Lohengrinades, I Prefer the Pyre!' · 1870–1880

In April 1870, at the request of the Egyptian government, Du Locle forwarded to Verdi a long printed opera scenario. He hinted that the author was well-known but wished to remain anonymous and explained that the Viceroy of Egypt (the Khedive) was looking for a suitable work for the Cairo Opera – if Verdi refused the commission he would approach Wagner or Gounod instead. Verdi noted that the text was extremely professional, though the subject matter was conventional and elements of the action closely resembled the current repertoire. The female protagonist, an Ethiopian slave called Aida, was an outsider like Ernani and Rigoletto, Azucena, and Violetta. However, the setting was unusual: Egypt at the time of the pharaohs.

Muzio had spent several months in Cairo conducting *Rigoletto* in 1869 (when the Suez Canal opened) and he told Verdi about the excellent facilities at the Cairo Opera, for the Khedive had invested a great deal of money in it. Verdi therefore demanded 150,000 francs (triple the sum he had received for *Don Carlos*), and then only for the exclusive rights in Egypt. The text had been written in French by Camille du Locle and based on a plot by the Egyptologist Auguste Mariette Bêy. Giuseppina helped Verdi with the Italian translation and Antonio Ghislanzoni (a Milanese journalist who had worked on the Italian version of *Don Carlos* and

In 1789, Napoleon's plans for a Suez Canal were abandoned when his engineer discovered the tidal disparity between the Mediterranean and the Red Sea. In 1855, Mougel, Linant and de Lesseps submitted a new scheme, and their canal opened in 1869.

the revision of *La forza del destino*) set it in verse. Verdi played a major role in shaping the libretto. He sent Ghislanzoni instructions almost daily, encouraging him to take *scenic liberties*, and pressing him to use *fewer words*[115] – and any he did use should be *parole scénique*: words suitable for the stage.[116] Auguste Mariette Bêy had sketched designs for statues, decorations, and costumes in an Egyptian style and Verdi, somewhat against his own principles, liked the idea of resurrecting an ancient culture. He unearthed information on instruments, dances, and religious rites under the pharaohs, and had a trumpet made (purely for visual effect) of the kind found in Egyptian tombs. Clearly he could not reconstruct the music, so he tried to find an exotic tone, particularly for the priestesses, using strange harmonies and static melodies full of minor and augmented seconds.

This time the subject matter was highly topical since anything exotic or oriental was all the rage. Other operas at the time included *L'Africaine* (*The African Woman*, 1837–64) by Meyerbeer, *Lakmé* (1833) by Léo Delibes (1836–91), and the Queen of Sheba, set as *La Reine de Saba* (1862) by Gounod, and *Die Königin von Saba* (1875) by Károly Goldmark (1830–1915). Painters had also flocked to Cairo, and in the 1860s group tours to the pyramids of El Ghiza became fashionable. The World Exhibition in Paris in 1867 had encouraged this mania for all things Egyptian. The general public admired the artefacts they saw exhibited, and looked to the opera stage for a reconstruction of these ancient religions, customs, and cultures, which appeared genuine even though they were merely created for a stage world of the imagination.

Aida was completed in November 1870, but the first performance had to be postponed because of the Franco-Prussian War – the costumes and scenery could not be shipped to Cairo via Paris as Paris was under siege. After the swift Prussian victory at Sedan, Verdi wrote to Clara Maffei: *This French catastrophe disheartens me, as it does you. It is true that French brag-ging, impertinence, and arrogance were and are intolerable, despite all their mis-fortunes. But when all is said and done, France has given freedom and civilisa-tion to the modern world. And if France falls, then let us not delude ourselves, our freedom and our civilisation will fall too.*[17] He was even moved to send

On 19 July 1870, war was declared between France and Prussia. After the Battle of Sedan on 1 September, Napoleon III gave himself up and the 'Second Empire' came to an end. Paris was invested two weeks later, but did not capitulate until 28 January, by which time King Wilhelm of Prussia had been proclaimed German Emperor at Versailles.

a contribution to Du Locle for the French war victims. It was not until Christmas Eve 1871 that a predominantly European audience saw the first performance of *Aida* at the Cairo Opera.

Contemporary illustration of *Aida* at the Cairo Opera

The lavish staging, the tableau presentation, and the massed scenes in the style of grand opéra, all enabled Verdi to fulfil the wishes of the Khedive for a suitably impressive spectacle. However, it is Verdi's exquisite handling of the orchestra that shows how highly ambitious this composition is from a technical point of view, although the opera still contains some traditional numbers. Continual instrumental themes point up the scenes; polyphonic composition creates many-layered references; the harmony is richer, and chromaticism and modulations are used to expand the tonal palette. Verdi creates recognisable patterns by repeating themes, two of which are combined contrapuntally in the prelude: Aida's gentle melody in the four-part divisi violins and the stiffly ceremonial fugal theme assigned to Ramfis and the Priests. Two themes clarify the inconsistency of the King's daughter, Amneris, one of which is moderato, demonstrating her elegance and self-possession, the other presto, often with variations, showing aggressive anxiety resulting from jealousy.

Opinions vary on the grand finale to Act 2, the so-called Triumphal Scene. Here the music, with its two orchestras and four choirs, provides impressive pomp to match the monumental staging. But this demonstration of military and religious power is only convincing if Verdi also intended to portray the arrogance of the ruling caste. When he proposed the text for the priests (*We have triumphed with the help of divine providence*) in a letter to Ghislanzoni,[118] Verdi was thinking of speeches by Wilhelm I, about whose delusions of grandeur he wrote to Clara Maffei: *that King who is continually quoting God and Divine Providence, and laying waste the best part of Europe with their help!*[119] The music does contain elements of criticism, in its all-pervasive and repetitive orchestral colouring, its powerful massed sound, and the mercilessness of the Priests' chorus. It is also evident when the (nameless) King, demanding hostages, obediently imitates the melody of the High Priests. However, these signals can make little headway against the gleaming gold of the stage, the animated rhythm of the triumphal march, the graceful song of the slave-girls, the dance of the little Moorish slaves, the ringing fanfares, and picturesque ballet. It is only Aida's cry of horror as she recognises her father among the prisoners that disturbs the celebrations; and only in the concertato, introduced by Amonasro's plea for mercy, that the suffering to come is indicated, before the chorus of homage, the salutations of the populace, and finally a repeat of the triumphal march bring the act to a festive close.

In the court scene the menace of the rulers is made quite clear. Verdi had never expressed his antipathy to the clergy so openly before. In the stark ritual formula of the accusations – stated three times, each at a higher pitch and becoming gradually more threatening – the individual is submerged. The anapaest rhythm of death in the formal address, three times repeated, *Radamès!* already contains the decision of the court; the judgement has been implicit from the beginning. This sense of utter hopelessness is shown in Radamès's silence when confronted by the united force of those in power, and in the helpless curse of Amneris on the *wicked race* of priests.

The qualities that unite all Verdi's operatic heroines are well-exemplified in Aida. She is *a stranger in this land*, like Elisabeth (see *Don Carlos*, Act 4, quartet); defenceless, as are all the lovers; beset by fear – evident in the broken lines of her aria, the *sprezzatura* typical of Verdi's women; homesick for another land; and always bidding farewell (note the similarity with Hélène's theme from the overture and the finale of Act 4 of *Les vêpres siciliennes*: *Adieu, mon pays*). Right from the start her singing is expressive of some unknown longing and grief, clearly evident in her repeated motif with which the prelude opens, and during her anticipation of happiness where it is combined with the death wish (Romance, Act 3), returning again in a vision of happiness as death approaches (Andantino, Act 4). The great melodic sweeps, spanning more than an octave, in remote keys, underlaid with seraphic notes in the orchestra, and revealing how thoughts and feelings attempt to

Amelia's prayer (*Un ballo in maschera*)

Elisabeth's aria (*Don Carlos*, Act 5)

Aida (final duet)

escape the confusions and struggles of their lives, are the hall-mark of other Verdi heroines.

The outdoor scene in Act 3 on the banks of the Nile at night is reminiscent of the sea at the opening of Act 1 of *Simon Boccanegra* (1856–7), with its dreamlike visualisation of a cherished hope. The sound of muted violins playing arpeggios without the mediant over a cello pedal and with a flute playing sounds from the natural world, combined with the static, almost bitonal moves between E minor and G minor, created the impression of a moon-lit land-scape, with distant singing to convey its expanse. Nature becomes an image of the *blessed, peaceful haven* of which Aida sings in her Romance *O cieli azzurri*, a homeland that can never be. The words *mai più* ('never again') are set on high C, and an oboe elegy laments how far distant is the fatherland. In the final scene, where the lovers have been buried alive, Aida defies the triumphant rulers in her song of farewell, sung in G-flat minor over an accompaniment by harp and flute, as if time stood still. She sings, like Luisa, Leonora, Gilda, and Violetta, of another world, and when her eyes are turned gently to the ground as she is dying in *O terra, addio* ('O earth, farewell'), with its persistent major seventh, she is thinking not of heaven but of that part of the earth which is her homeland.

On 8 February 1872, approximately two months after the première of Wagner's *Lohengrin* in Bologna, Verdi conducted his opera at La Scala with Teresa Stolz as Aida and Maria Waldmann as Amneris, two singers who were to triumph in these roles at other theatres too. Verdi insisted that the number of musicians in both chorus and orchestra should be augmented. He was not able to arrange for the orchestra to be lowered into a pit, as he had wished, following Wagner's example at Bayreuth. Under Verdi's baton *Aida* was a great success in Milan, Parma, Padua, Brescia, and Naples, thus enabling him to rescue several opera houses from financial ruin. The general level

Maria Waldmann, from a fresco in the Villa Massai-Ricasoli, Voghenza. The puritanical reaction against the excesses of the First Empire led to a cult in which women were regarded as muse, redeemer, and the embodiment of purity. Maria Waldmann, famous as Amneris in *Aida*, hovers like an angel above the earth in a high-necked dress that even covers her feet.

of performance had been sinking everywhere owing to low subsidies and high costs for singers and staging. According to Verdi, *Incredible negligence and ignorance* prevented reforms,[120] and it was even impossible to regulate concert pitch. He was horrified over and over again at how people distorted his operas. Thoughtless cuts were made, the tempi were not kept, sometimes sections were transposed down, and some numbers were completely altered.

Aida was soon known abroad and Verdi himself conducted

performances at the Paris Opéra. At last he received the unanimous praise he was due in that city; and yet, despite his international success, Verdi was angry and depressed. He had never paid much attention to either praise or criticism, but now he was distressed by some of the critical comments. *Aida* was 'coloured by German influences' wrote the French journalist Ernest Reyer after the première in Cairo, with no intention of denigrating it, rather as a term of respect; the contrapuntal elements, the tone colours, the harmonies and Verdi's orchestral score all showed that he had studied the works of Wagner. Reyer prophesied that Verdi would now 'win over many supporters, even in the circles from which he had been hitherto excluded'.[121] Naturally it did not escape Verdi's notice that the young intellectuals and critics were drawn increasingly to Wagner, whereas he was regarded in these fashionable circles as having been surpassed, falling behind Wagner's technical standard. This in itself deepened Verdi's mistrust of all schools, *systems, methods,* and *artistic terms.* He would *never become an academic musician,* but would *always remain a strummer;*[122] which is why, in 1879, he did not wish to become the honorary president of the orchestra at La Scala. He loathed the word 'Germanism'.

People were setting up chamber music clubs and orchestral societies everywhere at this time in order to educate the public in what was termed *high art.*[123] Verdi maintained that instead of imitating new trends from Germany, Italy should concentrate on its strength: vocal music. What he most admired in Shakespeare was valid for his own operas too: *to imitate truth is good, but to invent truth is better, much better.*[124] He was hurt that Wagner should be regarded as the only yardstick, and that *Aida* should be measured by this yardstick too. He wrote to De Sanctis in anger that he *never dreamed* that *Aida* would have anything in common with Wagner's music; it was *the opposite, the complete opposite.*[125] A year later he was complaining to his friend Tito Ricordi about the way in which the press was treating him: *stupid critics, and even more stupid praise: Not one thought worth mentioning on art, no one who tried to interpret my aims.*[126] He remained embittered for many years. In April 1875 he summed up his successes: *Endless discussion after* Aida *about how I was no longer the Verdi of* Un ballo in maschera . . . *that I did not understand how to write for singers . . . and that I just imitated Wagner!!! A fine result, to end a 35-year career as an imitator!!!*[127] He would not write another opera for 15 years.

The publicity for *Aida* in Cairo – *advertisements* for art as just a *business, a pleasure trip, a hunting party* – disgusted him. He associated them with the sensation that *Lohengrin* had caused in Italy. There were to be *no Lohengrinades for Aida – I would prefer the pyre!!!*[128] During a performance of *Lohengrin* in Bologna in 1871 Verdi had jotted down his impressions in the margins of a vocal score. He criticised many things as *ineffective* – the action dragged; many choruses

An 1879 caricature ridiculing the composer of *Aida* as a hurdy-gurdy player and imitator of Wagner.

were *boring*; the *organ style*; a lack of rhythm and concision; and, of course, the *hideous swan*. On the other hand he found some successes: the orchestration, for example, was *very beautiful*. His conclusion shows how much he mistrusted anything vague or mystical: *Beautiful music, when it is clear, has content.*[129] He later learned to appreciate *Lohengrin*; and he always regarded *Tristan und Isolde* as *one of the most sublime creations of the human spirit.*[130]

In April 1873 Verdi invited a few guests to his hotel in Naples. When they arrived they discovered to their surprise that music stands and candles had been set out. Slightly embarrassed, almost apologetic, Verdi humbly announced the performance of a string quartet he had written, merely to pass the time when rehearsals had been cancelled. It was not, however, merely an occasional piece of domestic music-making, and the choice of the quartet form reveals his desire to experiment with compositional techniques. Verdi's modesty was not feigned. It is shown equally in the unpretentious lay-out and the transparency of the writing in the four movements, which are for the most part to be played leggiero. A lyrical movement in sonata form is followed by a gentle mazurka, moving between the major and the minor and between remote keys. Following a bizarre scherzo there is a final fugue marked scherzo, but the countless chromatic and contrapuntal nuances leave no doubt about its compositional pretensions. Verdi hesitated for three years before he published his quartet, as it was *not a native Italian tradition*.[131]

'I am not at all sure how to thank you for your kind invitation to spend a few days with you in the country,' wrote the soprano Teresa

Writing in 1922, Verdi's fellow composer, Casella, wrote of his lone String Quartet, 'This work definitely warns the new generation that to persist in the operatic instrumental forms of the 19th century is to flog a dead horse, while, at the same time, it points out the new energetic cultivation of new forms . . . and it is well known that this example has already borne fruit.' Curiously, the quartet, whilst an acknowledged masterpiece, a great challenge for any ensemble, has never really taken its deserved place in the centre of the repertoire. Perhaps there is a suspicion that operatic composers cannot write chamber music, that steeped in orchestral and vocal technique, Verdi did not have the technical know-how to write comfortably for the quartet. John Dalley, violinist in the Guarneri quartet, complained of Verdi's tendency to write excessive amounts of *ppp*, a technique useful in keeping an orchestra quieter than singers in opera, but 'which are extremely difficult and uncomfortable to play in chamber music. Beethoven, on the other hand, writes *pp* in passages that are intrinsically suited to pianissimo interpretation.'

Stolz to Verdi in 1871. He fetched her from the railway station on 23 September and that same day Giuseppina recorded in her diary: 'Perhaps the saddest moment of my life. Signora Stolz arrived today. Beautiful as ever. Darkness, darkness, darkness stretches before me . . .'[132] This was not the first or only time that Giuseppina felt her husband was behaving in a thoroughly hurtful and insensitive manner. Sometimes he could be so cold towards her that she felt 'as if she were not there at all'.[133]

Born in Elbekosteletz in Prague in 1834, Teresa Stolz (real name Terezie Stolzovà) had been singing on the Italian stage since 1864. She was promoted by Mariani, to whom she had become engaged two years previously. At that time she had achieved great success in the part of Leonora in *La forza del destino* at La Scala. After her visit to the Verdis in September 1871 she broke off her engagement and became a frequent guest at Sant'Agata and at the Palazzo Sauli in Genoa, often staying for weeks on end. Giuseppina kept her feelings to herself and was kind to Stolz, in the belief, perhaps, that disaster could be averted if they became friends. But, as she confessed to Clara Maffei, Verdi's interest in this woman almost 20 years younger than her left her full of 'sadness, not to say despair',[134] and on the subject of her rival's correspondence with her husband she complained bitterly: 'Sixteen letters! In such a short time! How industrious . . .'[135] Even before her sixtieth birthday, Giuseppina was beginning to feel her age. She was convinced she had lost her looks and was merely living 'on memories'.[136] Frequently ill, she thought about death a great deal, and was also beginning to waver in her faith.

Verdi, on the other hand, now at the height of his fame, appeared to have more energy than he had shown in a long time. The flattering attentions of a younger woman helped him forget his age, and his wife reports that he responded to her suffering with 'hard, strong, hurtful words'[137] – the lack of consideration

Teresa Stolz, 1870

of someone who is head over heels in love.

Stolz stayed in the same hotel as the Verdis during rehearsals for *Aida* and for the *Requiem* in Paris; later also in Vienna and even when they went to the spa in Tabiano; and they always took their meals together. At one point in 1876, in Paris, Giuseppina drafted a letter to her husband in her diary: 'It did not seem to me to be the most fitting day to visit a lady who is neither your wife nor your daughter nor your sister . . . Think occasionally that I, your wife, who paid no attention to gossip in the past, am at this moment living in a *ménage à trois*, and that I have a right, if not to your love, at least to your respect.'[138]

In September the previous year a series of 'revelatory articles' had appeared in the Florentine *Rivista indipendente*. After various items of nasty gossip about Stolz's career there followed a sensational, extremely detailed report of an intimate relationship with Verdi. It is not certain whether Giuseppina knew of this article, though it is probable since she had asked De Sanctis about rumours concerning Verdi and Stolz three years previously, with the request that he reply in English. But in the end she maintained a united front when meeting her rival. She herself had been the victim of malicious gossip too. When Stolz retired from the stage in 1877, at the age of 43, the crisis seemed to be over, and some sort of friendship developed between the two women.

Verdi was deeply depressed when he learned of the death of Alessandro Manzoni in May 1873. The epoch that both he and Manzoni had represented was drawing to a close. Mariani died three weeks after Manzoni, but it was two years before Verdi would admit that this *poor man* – he could not bring himself to say Mariani's name – *was without doubt worth more than all the others put together.*[139] After Mariani's death the Verdis moved to new winter quarters in Genoa: a 20-room apartment in the Palazzo Doria.

Verdi wanted to write a Requiem Mass in homage to Manzoni to be performed in the Cathedral of San Marco in Milan on the first anniversary of his death. Apart from several very early works and the *Libera me* for the Pasticcio Mass in memory of Rossini, Verdi had composed no sacred music. He felt he had suffered much injustice from the clergy in Busseto, and his mistrust had grown over the years. He had shown – in the figure of the Grand Inquisitor in *Don Carlos* and the role of the priests in *Aida* – how power could be abused in the name of religion. The dogma of papal infallibility of 1870 only reinforced his antipathy to the Pope. Verdi was not a pious man; he was 'obstinate' in his agnosticism. Giuseppina considered him one of those 'who are content not to have faith, but who adhere to a strong moral code'.[140] Half in earnest and half ironically, Verdi wrote of his *Requiem*: *It seems to me that I have become a serious human being, no longer the public clown who cries 'Roll up! Roll up!' to the beat of the drum.*[141]

Verdi's advanced technique is shown in the polyphony, in the rich dissonance of the harmony, in the spaciousness of the instrumentation, and in the unity of his musical material. The compositional technique of the *Sanctus* is particularly remarkable, in that it develops two themes in its exposition, a sort of double fugue and a further staccato theme in the strings, into an almost dance-like cry of joy, the main theme rising like a fanfare. The extended final fugue of the *Libera me* is also fast (marked agitato), developing the theme with entirely dramatic impetus by means of inversions, strettos, modulations, and sequences. The *Requiem* for Manzoni is almost on the scale of an opera. Some 100 instrumentalists and 120 choral singers took part in the first performance, plus four soloists, including Teresa Stolz and Maria Waldmann, for whose voices the soprano and mezzo-soprano parts were written. Verdi wrote the work in his own musical language, without trying to modify it or include any of the antiquated, classical, or liturgical intonation which would have been foreign to his style. The *Dies irae* is related to the storm scenes in *Rigoletto* and *Otello*; the dark key of B minor and the first seven notes of the *Lacrymosa* are taken from a duet in *Don Carlos*, which was later cut, the lament of King Philippe for Posa; the glorious high strings from *La traviata* and *Aida* return briefly in the *Lux aeterna*. And when, at the beginning of the *Libera me*, the soprano sings in continuous, rushed, broken phrases (*senza misura*, and with a *dark voice*, almost whispering) we are reminded of Lady Macbeths's sleepwalking scene. The way in which the voices whisper, scream, and cry ('crying' is one of the directions in the *Lacrymosa*) adds an almost metaphysical aspect to this Mass. While the *Dies irae* becomes the dominant part of the

Requiem – it constitutes over half the work, and its main theme returns in the *Libera me* – the presentation of man's suffering, his torments, and his hope of salvation become the central focus of the work. (Many years later, Jewish prisoners sang Verdi's *Requiem* in the Theresienstadt concentration camp in Czechoslovakia.) Never before had Verdi depicted collective fear with such force: sudden dramatic tuttis, lashing scales for the wind, the choir like one four-part scream of pain. The terror of the *Tuba mirum*, the curse motif of the *Rex tremendae*, and the annihilating power of the *Confutatis* are contrasted with the many laments, sighs, and sounds of pain (*Quid sum miser*), the powerlessness of the individual, the hesitant singing, and the speechless horror before the abyss (*Mors stupebit*). The cry for liberation in the *Libera me* – punctuated with brutal orchestral gestures and accompanied by trumpet fanfares and drum rolls – sounds almost like an ultimatum. Whatever form liberation may take, the Mass closes with the quietest *piano*, withdrawing into a liturgical tone, like a whispered prayer.

Arrigo Boito, a member of the city council, acted as intermediary so that the ceremony of remembrance could take place on 22 May 1874, despite fierce opposition on account of the high cost. Three days later Verdi conducted his Mass at La Scala and it was performed shortly afterwards in many other Italian opera houses and abroad. The German conductor Hans von Bülow (1830–94) found Verdi's 'newest opera in church vestments' embarrassing. His attack on this 'Roman barbarism' in the *Allgemeine Zeitung*, accusing it of being 'full of bad taste and ugliness',[142] provoked an angry counter-attack in the Italian press. A year later Verdi's critics in Germany and elsewhere were of a completely different opinion. Even sworn opponents of Verdi were united in their praise for the *Requiem*. Eighteen years later Bülow apologised for his 'great journalistic blunder'. He conceded that Verdi's last works – *Aida*, the *Requiem*, and *Otello* – had moved him to tears.[143]

HANS VON BÜLOW

Since the *Requiem* had proved such a money-spinner, people arranged it for various ensembles – even a military band, much to Verdi's disgust. He complained to his publisher about it and also bemoaned several incompetent performances. He felt as if he were *a worker, a hack, who delivered his wares to a firm and the firm distributed them just as it pleased.*[144]

In 1877 Verdi conducted his *Requiem* in Cologne at the Rhineland Music Festival with 700 musicians. The composer and conductor Ferdinand Hiller (1811–85) had invited him, and they continued a correspondence thereafter. Verdi almost envied Hiller, who was two years older, for his activity. *The older I get, he wrote, the more I desire to do nothing . . . I am rather ashamed and regretful about this.*[145] Fame was little consolation in old age. Aged 60 he wrote to Clara Maffei about his deep depression: *I believe in nothing any more, in nobody, almost . . . I have suddenly experienced such great and horrid disappointments.*[146] His long-standing friendship with the De Sanctis family had been damaged by the non-repayment of loans; there were similar grounds for a break with Escudier; Verdi had claims for outstanding payments against Du Locle, who, as director of the Opéra-Comique, had come to grief financially. In 1876 two of Verdi's old friends, Piave and Luccardi, died. He took some comfort, however, when young people, such as the singer Maria Waldmann, wrote to him saying that they were *thinking of their old maestro.* Verdi replied to her in July 1876: *You are young, beautiful, and now at the very peak of happiness. Here we are living quietly, and if life is not exactly cheerful, it is nevertheless tolerable.*[147] It did the Verdis good to have their adopted daughter Filomena with them. She had successfully completed her training as a primary school teacher in Turin (in which Giuseppina had had a hand), and Verdi remarked that the two women were *forever talking.*[148] When Filomena (or Fifao, as she was known) married Alberto Carrara in 1878 it provided a good excuse to renovate the Villa Sant'Agata once again.

Portrait of Giuseppina Verdi in the Villa Sant'Agata. 'She spoke very simply, rather slowly, not from inhibition but with care, so that she seemed almost to be sifting her few but apposite words and phrases . . . any judgement she passed in the form of a doubt.'[149]

This winter there will be price increases and famine once more, Verdi prophesied in 1879 after a dreadful flood when the River Po broke its banks. *And,* he added, *at the same time the Government is thinking of raising taxes.*[150]

Verdi conducted his *Requiem* at a benefit concert at La Scala for the flood victims and raised 37,000 lire. Many farmers and other workers in his close neighbourhood had suffered as a result of the war, and he very generously helped them for many years with money, food, and advice. For a while there was even a food kitchen for the poor at Sant'Agata. Verdi also provided financial support for musicians in distress, including the young composer Ruggiero Leoncavallo (1857–1919) among others. Verdi was bitter about the continuing economic crisis, the incompetence of the various governments, the colonial policy, and the insignificance of Italy in the realm of foreign policy.

Verdi's life work seemed to have come to an end with the *Requiem*. When he was 66 he dictated part of his autobiography to Ricordi, at the latter's request. Giuseppina envisaged that the Palazzo Cavalli would become a memorial to Verdi. After the successful première of *Aida* in Paris she wrote to her husband from Genoa: 'The ovations can rise to the heavens, but let me come to you. You will see that I will not disturb you, but just tell you quietly and movingly how much I love and respect you, while others are silent as they catch their breath and blow their noses.'[151] In 1880 she accompanied her husband to Milan where he was made an honorary citizen. The King conferred on him the title of Knight of the Grand Cross of the Italian Crown. During the celebrations both of his new sacred pieces were sung: the *Ave Maria* for soprano and string orchestra, and the *Pater Noster* for five-part a cappella choir, which sounded like a homage to the Italian composer Palestrina.

'What if I never reach the end of my music?' · 1879–1901

Years passed in the same routine. Verdi and Giuseppina spent the winters in Genoa where they celebrated Christmas with Muzio, De Amicis and his wife, and Teresa Stolz, who had her own apartment there. From time to time Verdi travelled from Genoa to Sant'Agata to see to the rent-payments, the purchase of seed, repairs, and new building work. He employed a total of 200 agricultural and construction workers and at one time had 16 people labouring on the gardens alone.[152] The Verdis spent the spring and late summer in Sant'Agata, often inviting friends and acquaintances. Muzio, Boito, Stolz, and Giuseppina's sister, Barberina, often stayed for several weeks. Verdi enjoyed having guests. He showed them his library, his collections of old prints and rare manuscripts, made sure the meals were excellent, and occasionally cooked. In the evenings they played cards or billiards. For the most part they maintained their normal everyday routines. While Verdi was busy with his various works, the guests treated the house *as if they had been living there for ten years*. Verdi seldom played them his own music on the piano, though one visitor remembered how he once read aloud passages from the *Otello* libretto with plenty of fire and dramatic characterisation. On one summer evening in the garden, Stolz, Boito, and Giuseppe Giacosa (a writer and friend of Boito's) sang arias from *Ernani* in the twilight, then ran through whole scenes, while Verdi's Giuseppina sat watching on the stone steps, laughing and applauding.[153]

An interior view of Sant'Agata. A portrait of Verdi hangs on the wall. The marble bust is a likeness of the young Giuseppina Strepponi

In June or July the Verdis set off for the spas of Tabiano or Montecatini, together with Stolz and the two De Amicis. Their routine was broken only by visits to Paris, where Verdi conducted *Aida* in 1880; in 1882 he was negotiating copyright; and in 1886 he went with his wife and Muzio to hear the French baritone Victor Maurel (1848–1924). He made his last visit to Paris when he was 80. They visited Milan regularly, at least once a year, often in April, and admired the glass-vaulted Galleria Vittorio Emanuele, with its countless elegant shops and restaurants, which was built in 1877. Here the Verdis lived in the Grand Hôtel Milan, in 'their' suite, and met their 'musical Round Table': the Ricordis, Faccio, Boito, Clara Maffei, and Teresa Stolz – who received visitors on Mondays in her 'Egyptian salon' (in homage to *Aida*) and often organised concerts.

One evening, during dinner in Milan with Ricordi and a few other friends, the conversation turned by chance to Rossini's *Otello* (1816). Just three days later Arrigo Boito brought over his sketch of a libretto for *Otello*. This was in 1879, seven years before the first performance of Verdi's opera. Since he had offended Verdi so deeply with his 'Ode to Italian Art', the sensitive Boito had refrained from suggesting a collaboration until Giulio Ricordi intervened. Boito wrote stories as well as libretti, and translated a great deal, including several texts by Wagner. He had been writing an opera, *Nerone*, for more than 15 years (it was still incomplete when he died in 1918), and had caused a scandal in 1868 with his opera *Mefistofele*, although its revival in 1875 was a triumph. Now, however, he had nothing but *Otello* in his head. He delivered the libretto three months later. Verdi bought it and filed it among his papers. The slightest hint of an obligation put Verdi off, and he fought shy of such a large task (he had never managed to finish *Re Lear*); added to which there was considerable pressure on him to rival Wagner, and he wondered how much time was left to him. In the end, however, Verdi was drawn 'into the net, more or less blindly and against his will', as Giuseppina confided to Ricordi.[154] Naturally Ricordi wanted a new opera by Verdi, but he knew the composer well enough to treat him with kid gloves. He agreed with Giuseppina that they would maintain absolute silence about the 'Moor'. The only exception he made was that, after 1881, the Christmas cake he sent every year to the Verdis was always decorated with a little chocolate figure of a Moor with his legs missing.

Verdi first requested Boito's help on a new version of a work he had written 23 years before. *I am in the process of mending the legs of an old dog which was thrashed in Venice, and which is called Simon Boccanega*, he wrote to Arrivabene in 1881.[155] Boito improved on Piave's libretto while Verdi composed an almost impressionistic prelude and drafted a new scene for Act 1 with a speech by the Doge to the warring people of Genoa – a ringing appeal for reconciliation that reflected the political and social tensions of Verdi's own day. Although the new version of *Simon Boccanegra* was well received on

24 March 1881, this opera with its dark colours and the difficulty of casting its lead parts never became as popular as Verdi's great successes of the early 1850s.

The following year Verdi shortened *Don Carlos* to four acts. *Operas that are too long get savagely amputated*, he wrote to Piroli. *When they decided to cut off my legs, I preferred to sharpen and wield the knife myself.* [156] He remained sceptical after the successful première of this new version of *Don Carlos* in Milan in January 1884. *Those clapping hands should be saying: 'You're still alive, and so old – play us something to dance to, even if it wears you out!'* [157]

Verdi's views on music at this time almost always sound angry: *I am not discussing anything; I don't know anything, and I don't want to know anything.* [158] Although his library was full of music – and in 1885 Muzio had sent him the scores from Paris of Wagner's *Die Meistersinger von Nürnberg* and *Parsifal* (1877–82) – Verdi maintained that he was against progress. He hid behind the mask of an ignorant farmer who trusts his own instincts and he almost always declined to pass judgement on other composers. Behind his insistence on simplicity and naturalness (as befits a farmer) and his objection to anything artificial or excessive, he was sensitive as an artist to certain dangers ahead, in particular signs of national decline as the century drew to a close. He was unhappy that the young composers in Italy were *being infected by the French* or *German disease* [159] and were only composing *à la Chopin, à la Mendelssohn, à la Gounod, etc.* [160] The first opera by the young Italian composer Puccini, *Le Villi*

Warsaw-born Fryderyk Chopin's (1810–49) uniquely expressive piano style quietly revolutionised the expressive range of his instrument, through his 2 concerti, and particularly his Nocturnes and 24 Preludes. Upon first hearing him, Schumann famously wrote, 'Hats off, gentlemen, a genius.' The Parisian crictics crowned him 'Ariel of the Piano.' He lived with the novelist George Sand from 1838–1947 before succumbing to tuberculosis. She depicted him unflatteringly in her novel *Lucrezia Floriani*. Chopin's Broadwood piano is in the collection of the Royal Academy of Music, London.

(*The Willis*), was performed in Milan in May 1884, and after this rather romantic debut Ricordi became Puccini's champion and publisher. Verdi also expressed approval: *He is following the modern trend, which is natural, but he remains close to his melody, which is neither modern nor old-fashioned. The symphonic element seems predominant in his work. This is no disadvantage, but it must be treated with care. Opera is opera, symphony is symphony, and I do not recommend inserting a symphonic piece into an opera merely to let the orchestra dance.*[161] Puccini's later operas do not seem to have interested Verdi, since he expressed no further opinions on this composer in his letters.

The Italian composer Giacomo Puccini (1858–1924), was the fifth generation of a distinguished family of musicians. He showed no real enthusiasm for music as a child, and it was not until he heard a performance of *Aida* in Pisa in 1876 that he determined to become an opera composer; to this end, he studied with Bazzini and Ponchielli at the Milan Conservatory. Ricordi heard his opera Le Villi, in Milan in 1884, and commissioned *Edgar* for La Scala. True success and acclaim was only his with the premier of *Manon Lescaut* in Turin in 1893. His last opera, *Turandot*, was produced shortly after his death from cancer in 1926.

Exhausted from his theatre work, Verdi suffered an attack of fatigue in April 1883. He could not bear inactivity, so he now concentrated all his energies on practical matters: the hay, grain, and grape harvests; breeding cattle and horses; necessary repairs; the ordering of new harnesses; the settling of bills. In 1880 he had had a dairy built, primarily to create work for the local people. He was proud of the fact that there was no unemployment in his area and that nobody had been forced to leave. He was also planning to build a small hospital in Villanova. *The poor patients in this district only have the hospital in Piacenza which is 34 or 36 kilometres away, and most of these patients die on the way there,* he reported to Piroli.[162] Construction began in the spring of 1883, and the hospital was opened five years later.

Verdi's recurring bouts of depression show how much he was

missing his music. In October 1883 Clara Maffei received a dejected letter from him: *I believe that life is entirely stupid, and worse, useless. What is to be done? What can we do? All in all, there is just one shaming, desolate answer: NOTHING!*[163] He felt old and tired. Then, in December 1884, he finally began to work seriously on the composition of *Otello*. He started a letter to Boito with a cry of joy: *I am writing!! I am writing!! . . . without worrying about what happens later.*[164] 'Later' meant *all the publicity,* which he never liked and which was almost *hateful* to him as he grew older.[165]

Verdi was able to work more intensively with Boito than he had with any other librettist. However, his respect for Boito's competence and erudition did not prevent him from making continual suggestions. He knew Shakespeare's tragedy, *Othello, the Moor of Venice* (1602–4) extremely well from constant re-reading and he took a keen interest in the form the libretto should take. Boito, who put himself completely at Verdi's service, and who always addressed him in his letters as 'Maestro', regarded their collaboration as an honour; he accepted Verdi's guidance and suggestions with unusual musical understanding.

When Verdi repeatedly wondered aloud if he would ever finish *Otello*, it was not just to stimulate public curiosity. His doubts were deep-seated and never left him all the time he was composing. There was the constant fear that he would not reach the end. *Everything is disturbing and upsetting, and time is lost! Oh, Time!!*[166] At one point work ceased for months on end because Verdi was exhausted. Then time dragged and he felt as if each day were a *vacuum.*[167] Nevertheless, on 1 November 1886, Boito received a message from Verdi: *It is finished! All praise to us . . . (and also to HIM!!)*[168] But by then two of Verdi's oldest friends and most trusted confidants were no longer alive: Clara Maffei had died in July 1886, followed by Opprandino Arrivabene three months later, and Verdi was sad that they would never see the first performance.

No journalists or visitors were allowed into the rehearsals, which Verdi impatiently supervised, almost always discontented. This secrecy only whetted the public's appetite even more and there was much interest in and excitement about Verdi's new opera. The management of La Scala was besieged by requests for tickets from all over the world. By noon on the day of the première (5 February 1887) the streets in Milan were blocked with people and traffic, and there were constant shouts of 'Viva Verdi!' outside the opera house. The principal singers were Francesco Tamagno (Otello), Romilda Pantaleoni (Desdemona), and the famous Victor Maurel (Iago), with Franco Faccio (1840–91) conducting. Afterwards Giuseppina reported 'deafening applause, ending in frenzy'.[169] Verdi invited Boito on to the stage, and the younger man never forgot how Verdi had seized his hand: 'his touch – there was something so kind, so paternal, so protective about it.'[170] Outside La Scala people had unharnessed the horses from Verdi's carriage in order to pull him themselves to his hotel, where they played music beneath his windows all night long. *Never again*, so Verdi believed, would he experience such joy at a work he had completed – and with that *never again* it seemed to him a *death knell* had sounded along with all the shouts of joy.

Otello opens with harsh dissonance and noises breaking over the audience, but it is not just the portrayal of a storm. Lashing glissandi (even for the trombones), rushing scales, triplets, unresolved dissonances, chromatic sequences of diminished seventh chords, plus thunderclaps, cannon shots, cries of fear and wailing horns (*come un lamento*), the chorus expressing their horror, and all of this over an organ cluster (C, C sharp, D) which is held for 256 bars. To reinforce the dark register of the orchestra, Verdi had a bass trombone constructed by the firm of Pelitti, who had also made the trumpets for *Aida*. The formless chaos becomes an allegory for human peril. *Now it is sinking, / Now it is being tossed*

Stage set for Scene 1 of the première of *Otello* at La Scala in Milan, 1887. The storm on which Shakespeare's characters only comment, is presented in three-and-a-half minutes of descriptive music with an intensity never heard before.

to the heavens, they sing about Otello's ship, and *the whole universe groans* like a scene from the apocalypse, as the men and women on the shore sing a sort of prayer before the first long chord – in E major, the key of the 'bacio' (kiss) motif – announces *He is safe!* When the restless triplets come to an end – and for a moment the ringing C sharp major of the *Esultate* heralds quite a different sound – Otello makes his first entrance, against the background of the storm, a victorious hero. It is against this heroic entrance that we measure his eventual fall, greater than that of any other of Verdi's heroes.

At first it was Shakespeare's villain who attracted Verdi's interest, and for a while the opera was to be called Iago. Verdi wanted to visualise his face, and pressed the painter Morelli to make a portrait of this evil ensign who persuades Otello that the innocent Desdemona has been unfaithful. Once Boito had been encouraged to write it, Verdi found Iago's *Credo magnificently realised* and he composed a travesty of an aria for this text: remnants of scena, cantabile, and cabaletta, with a disjointed syntax expressing the breakdown of his character (in contrast, Verdi had written a regular aria for Francesco Moor's blasphemous monologue in *I masnadieri*). Iago's evil streak had already been shown in the beva of the drinking song, with its chromatic melismas. The theatrical *Credo* shows how Iago's lack of personal identity is replaced by the power he usurps. Just how he is driven by his cynical desire first to humiliate the other characters, then to observe them like a voyeur, can be seen in the motifs expressing scorn (low trills, mocking brass notes, and triplets for the woodwind), and in the shape of the melodic lines. Iago enjoys his blasphemies, intoning over dissonant tremoli. His arrogance, terrifying and at the same time grotesque, can be heard in the massive unison of the orchestral ritornello, the use of glissandi as exclamation marks, and in the fanfare-like chords. This master of disguise appears in many other roles. At the moment when he warns Otello against jealousy, while the melody snakes sinuously over chromatic chords, the music quite clearly points up his falseness through its own exaggerations; and after the pathetic warning of Iago's *È un'idra*, in unison with the bass instruments, the close in popular ballad style with its strident trills shows up the impostor with perfect clarity. He demonstrates his skill once more in the telling of the dream, where he imitates endearments with a gently rocking siciliana in the limpid key of C major.

The other notable quality in this libretto, compared to those of earlier operas, is not just the poetry of the language, but also the many layers of the stage action. When Iago is arousing Otello's jealousy in Act 2, at the same time, interspersed with their dialogue, there is a chorus of homage in E major, the key of the 'bacio' motif

Verdi was fascinated by instrumental technology. His century witnessed an explosion in the development of wind and brass instrument, as had happened earlier with the string family. Impetus to this had been given by Napoleon, who demanded impressive military instruments resembling ancient Roman models. Composers were to the forefront of this development. Richard Wagner commissioned a special horn, the 'Wagner Tuba' to produce the sound he imagined for his opera cycle, and Verdi commissioned trumpets for Aida. These slim fanfare trumpets were modelled on Egyptian iconography. They fell into obsolescence, but the recent upsurge of interest in 19th-century 'performance practice' has led to their revival, spearheaded by conductors such as Nicholas Harnoncourt.

in the love duet, as Desdemona appears in the garden, surrounded by flowers that the islanders bring for her. This *ray of light amidst the darkness*,[171] almost a devotional image, suggests that all is not yet lost. In the third act, after the ship with the Venetian ambassadors has landed, Iago and Otello plot Desdemona's murder against the background of trumpets and cannons and a chorus of Vivas! for Otello, the *Lion of Venice*. This juxtaposition demonstrates clearly the depth of his fall, and to what extent reality and imagination have diverged.

Although the four acts each contain the customary numbers – drinking song (Act 1); Chorus of homage; soldiers' song; dream narration; oath; quartet (Act 2); concertato (Act 3); ballad and *preghiera* (Act 4) – these are now integrated into the action and are given new dramatic functions. An example of Verdi's method of combining individual scenes seamlessly together is the flowing transition in Act 1 from the chaos of drinking and fighting to the love duet. The music gradually calms down over a pedal point, while the solo cello and then the passage for four muted cellos with their gentle dominant ninths create a quiet space for the meeting that follows. Otello begins the dialogue almost in a trance, as does Desdemona in her reply, which is in a remote key accompanied only by muted strings. It is clear from the beginning that their love is threatened. They both remember the past, like people bidding each other farewell; they sing separately, without touching, and in Otello's cry of joy, in D flat minor, where his top note lies on *temo* ('I fear'), there is also fear in the music. The real love motif – the 'bacio' motif in E major – has only fragmentary words set to it. The boundlessness of this moment is set against the static music for the harps and high tremoli, unexpectedly in D flat major, unsupported by bass, and with the light of the starry sky as a backdrop.

The image of the hero, victor over the elements, the famous general whom Desdemona had greeted with the words *My splendid warrior!* is gradually destroyed. By the end, Otello is no longer even in command of himself. The subject of the opera is not really his jealousy caused by character and social circumstance. This Otello is, rather, an individual unsure of himself, searching for his own identity, the Moor, upstart and outsider, who is particularly susceptible to being led astray. A dark, distant march, accompanied by open chords on the harp, against which Otello takes his leave of all that was most important in his life hitherto, his life as a soldier, signals just how broken his image of himself has now become. This loss of confidence, this fear of living in a world of deception, lead to his forceful and at the same time helpless attempts to discover the truth. Desdemona's oath should reassure him: *Tell me who you are!* The beginning and the end of their dialogue in the third act, their greeting and their parting, are again in E major. Grace and a distant formality, love and mistrust, are all contained in the way in which the two address each other. The beauty of the music, a gentle cantilena with graceful melismas, is broken by Otello's threats and his fearful accusation. When, however, the E major tune of the beginning is reintroduced at the end, the da capo acquires new meaning. Otello is no longer singing *con eleganza* but with the most terrible quiet irony. What the music had hinted at the outset has now become a certainty. It breaks out into harsh dissonance as carefully controlled emotions are dispersed in the postlude, and the chromatic rise and fall reveals the impossibility of Otello's position: with the loss of Desdemona he has lost himself.

A disquieting low note on the double basses, an E following the A flat major of the *Ave Maria* immediately preceding it, introduces Otello's last entrance. His inner feelings are sketched with just a few motifs: his desolate grief in the double bass melody and later on the cor anglais; his suppressed agitation in the broken staccato figures for the violas; his fearful certainty of approaching disaster in the recurring low notes for the wind. These motifs run through the whole scene until, with Desdemona's cry of fear, dissonances are heard like hammer blows – a disturbing sound effect, reminiscent of the storm at the beginning. The opera ends without a reconciliation. Desdemona dies without a vision, and Otello's end is equally hopeless. As he realises the truth, in his first glimpse of his dead wife, the orchestra quotes the 'bacio' theme in its original E major for the last time: he sees the awful truth and what he has irrevocably lost.

On my desk it was a comfort, now it is a hell! Verdi complained to his publisher when he heard of the inadequate staging for *Otello* in various opera houses.[172] Despite successes in Vienna under Hans Richter, and in London, he remained bitter about these poor productions, which all seemed to confirm what the critics were continually *stating loudly: that genuine, sublime music drama ... is to be found in Germany and France* but not in Italy, as Verdi complained to Ricordi in 1892.[173] The customary ballet was required for the Paris Opéra, which Verdi found an *artistic monstrosity*.[174] He very

Hans Richter (1843–1916) became principal conductor of the Vienna Court Opera in 1875, where he also conducted the Philharmonic Orchestra from 1875–97. Having worked as von Bülow's chorus master at the Munich Opera, he conducted the Bayreuth première of Wagner's Ring cycle in 1876. Upon leaving the Vienna Philharmonic, he took over the reins of the Hallé Orchestra in Manchester, and also conducted the London Symphony from 1904–11. He was an early champion of the works of Sir Edward Elgar.

nearly asked that someone else be given the task of composing it, but eventually did it himself.

Boito observed how much Verdi missed writing music in later life. A competition in the Milan *Gazzetta musicale* to set a musical conundrum, a *scala enigmatica*, spurred the almost 75-year-old composer to write an *Ave Maria* over this cantus firmus. 'Ave Marias are not enough. You need something more,' insisted Boito. 'There is only one way of making a better ending than *Otello*, and that would be to end in triumph with *Falstaff*.'[175] The plan for this new opera arose out of a conversation between the two men in May 1889. The sources on which Boito drew – Shakespeare's *King Henry IV* Parts 1 and 2 (*c*.1597); *Henry V* (1599); and *The Merry Wives of Windsor* (*c*.1602) – were familiar to Verdi from his own reading, as were the plays of Italy's greatest comic dramatist Carlo Goldoni (1707–93). Verdi had considered a comic subject for an opera before, angered by a remark of Rossini's in 1879 that Verdi was a composer of tragedies who would never write a comic opera. But although Verdi wanted to compose *Falstaff*, he had more scruples than ever before: *What happens if I can't overcome my weakness?! . . . What if I can't finish writing the music?* But the decision was made. *What fun to be able to say to the general public: 'Here we are again!! Roll up!!'* [176] *Falstaff* was a much greater gamble than *Otello*. It was a *commedia lirica* with original characters in place of comic stereotypes and with closed numbers in a conversational style, rather than the stock comedy situations of *opera buffa*; while its reflective, even melancholy aspects placed it outside any traditional form. The last repertoire Italian *opera buffa*, Donizetti's *Don Pasquale*, was first performed in 1843.

The project was kept secret for almost a year and a half, as Verdi was afraid to commit himself. At a dinner in Milan in 1890 Boito mischievously proposed a strange toast, which puzzled Verdi's guests. He drank 'to the health and success of fatso (*pancione*)'.[177] The following day Milan papers carried news of a new opera. For

Verdi relaxing in the garden at Sant'Agata. His devotion to the estate was all-consuming, at one time he employed 16 gardeners to tend the grounds

his part, Verdi was concerned that Boito was neglecting his own opera, *Nerone*, in favour of *Falstaff*. He was continually urging Boito to persevere with *Nerone*. Writing Falstaff was a great challenge to the elderly composer and Verdi let the work fall off from time to time. By 1891 the manuscript had been left untouched for many months. This was partly a result of the difficulties he had to cope with at the Villanova hospital: insufficient staff, constant interventions from the priests, and at one time inadequate nursing, which Verdi found especially difficult to tolerate. He patiently answered all of his letters and dealt with everything. *I am in rather a muddle and out of sorts . . . the sad events of the last few months, the cold weather at the moment, the festivities of the season etc. etc. have upset my equilibrium,* he wrote to Boito at the beginning of 1891.[178] He was increasingly conscious of his age. His old friend Piroli had died in November 1890. Two weeks later came the death of Muzio, who had seemed terribly altered the previous year from liver disease, but his last will and testament demonstrated once again his everlating devotion to his 'Maestro'. Verdi's worries were compounded by anxiety about Giuseppina, whose health was visibly deteriorating. She suffered from arthritis and could hardly walk from pains in her joints. Both of them were depressed by the disaster that had overtaken Faccio, who had for many years shown evidence of brain damage caused

Emanuele Muzio, Verdi's only pupil, became well known outside Italy as an energetic conductor. He was *good-hearted, but not endowed with the capacity to understand either himself or the world*, Verdi wrote to Clara Maffei in 1848.[179] In later years, when Muzio was enjoying success in London, New York, and Paris, Verdi continued to care for him like an elder brother.

SICKNESS

by syphilis. When he was threatened with redundancy by La Scala, Verdi arranged for him to be offered the position of director of the Conservatory in Parma, which had just become vacant, but he was too ill to take this up. Boito looked after his friend selflessly, offering him his own salary, taking care of doctors and treatment until it became necessary for Faccio to enter a sanatorium, where he died in the summer of 1891. *Everything is coming to an end!!* wrote Verdi at the time. This thought was sometimes so overwhelming that not even music could distract him from it. *I am writing aimlessly, just simply to pass a few hours in the day,* he reported to Maria Waldmann.[180]

In the winter of 1891–2 Verdi and his wife had very bad influenza, which meant he was unable to work for a long time. *I will read Job again,* he wrote in one letter.[181] At home, illness seemed the only subject of conversation. Giuseppina, who was in constant pain, had acquired a medical encyclopaedia from Milan. Even her sister Barberina, who often stayed with them, was continually ill. In April 1892 Verdi was persuaded to conduct the prayer from Rossini's *Mosé in Egitto* (*Moses in Egypt*) at La Scala to celebrate the centenary of the composer's birth, but there was still the question of his comic opera to attend to. *Will I ever finish what I have to do? . . . At this moment I feel so tired, so listless,* he wrote in May 1892 to Boito, who was already busy with sketches for the costumes.[182] But then, his enthusiasm for the subject renewed, he began to work in earnest again and finished the score at the end of September.

Falstaff may be an old-fashioned, run-down knight, with his best years long behind him, a *pancione*, a glutton and a self-centred parasite, but his confrontation with the citizens of Windsor turns him into an operatic hero. He continually provokes them until they eventually turn on him. In a way, he helps them to gain a better understanding of themselves by inspiring them to join in the game, to see the poetry in every situation. And in the end it is Falstaff who triumphs: *I am the one who has tricked you* – to be sung *quietly, gently, dolce*. This is followed immediately by the electrifying fortissimo chord with which the opera opens and which permeates the music in a number of variations. Here it throws everything into confusion.

The second theme, on the other hand, presents the noble rogue in all his youthful grace, expressed in his song about his time as a page (*Quand'ero paggio*). Even his deceitful tricks are not without charm. If you have to steal in this inhospitable world, he cautions his servants, then at least do it with *elegance*. His massive belly is a metaphor for his appetite for life, and his greatest pleasure, lust, requires no moral or religious justification. Aware that he is getting no younger and afraid that he will end his days in poverty, he woos two fair Windsor beauties simultaneously. And love gives wings to his imagination: when he courts Alice in a ridiculously elaborate and old-fashioned manner; when he lauds the image of the future Lady Falstaff, caricatured in high parallel octaves on the bassoon and flute; when he plays out a dramatic scene and imitates the object of his desire in a comic falsetto. In Falstaff's moral sermon to his servants exemplifying *honour*, he uses the empty words of conventional morality, as he repeatedly replies with a dry *No* to their false pathos. The multiple, mocking trills in the wind are reminiscent of Iago's *Credo*. Falstaff's maxim is, however, a trite march – *Va, vecchio John* – is an affirmation of life; he is at one with himself and his thorough-going enjoyment of life can be heard in the instrumental commentary.

Even when, at the start of Act 3, Falstaff is half dead, soaked to the skin, and humiliated, complaining that the world has gone to the dogs, his maxim comes through, this time as a funeral march. The monologue begins with a curse (*Mondo ladro*), and here again the rising figure, intoned on the low wind instruments, is reminiscent of the curse motifs in earlier Verdi operas. His grand gesture is, however, taken back to piano and pianissimo. Falstaff ends by being subdued, depressed that he has grown so old. But wine revives him, as the orchestra demonstrates. Wine sets everything in motion again: first the flutes, then more and more instruments, and finally even the trombones begin to trill in many harmonic colours, until, in this musical allegory on the creative power of alcohol, the whole world appears to have become one single trill – although Mistress Quickly's *Reverenza* soon sobers him up.

The people of Windsor hunt down Falstaff, first in Ford's house then at midnight in the park (Act 2, Scene 2), where they torment him like an animal and their mood turns vicious (Wagner used a similar thrashing in *Die Meistersinger*); but Verdi's portrait of the citizens of Windsor has its lighter touches: they are amiable folk who take no malicious pleasure in Falstaff's discomfiture. Only the young lovers rise above the rest. The few moments in which Nannetta and Fenton are alone are like film flashbacks, differentiated in harmony, tempo, and rhythm, a gentle legato for the strings and woodwind; plus the lyrical tone of the singers, whose alternating voices build one single melodic line. These moments, are, however, only a fleeting reminder of the traditional love duet. And as it is love itself about which they sing – the *beautiful game*, always new – the quotation from Boccaccio's *Decameron* (1349–51) is repeatedly woven into their song (*Bocca baciata*) emphasising an impression of timelessness.

Dr Cajus and Ford, discontented, nervous, and unselfconfident characters, worry about their *possessions*, which for them consist of *honour, house*, and *bed*, which must be *preserved from the appetites of strangers*. Ford, however, disguised as Master Brook, is able to free himself, and he descends into melting pathos as he sings of his own wife; while under the contagious influence of Falstaff's love he warbles with his rival *L'amor, l'amor*. The manner in which

Alice reads aloud the flowery ending of Falstaff's letter *dolcissimo* and with gushing suspended ninths reveals unacknowledged desire despite the caricatures of her final trills and the ensuing laughter.

Once the hunt is over a general reconciliation is made in the final fugue, which brings all the voices together. Falstaff announces the theme, and engages the others to reflect on recent events for a minute before they start the banquet. It is again Falstaff who 'discovers' the inversion of the theme, as it returns for the penultimate time, before all the voices are overcome by laughter and come to a halt on a chord of the seventh. After the subdued admission *Tutti gabbati* ('We are all figures of fun'), the fugue ends in general laughter. This concertante ending, in which the singers step out of their roles, demonstrates the play within a play, and is a homage

The score for the female soloists at the beginning of Scene 2 of *Falstaff* is notable for the handling of the voices in the ensemble. The mosaic of notes builds into a single melody, to be compared with the *fragmentary nature* of the orchestral score.

to Mozart, whose *Don Giovanni* ends with a fugue. A further reference to this opera is the minuet for the masked revellers in the third act, while the nocturnal use of masks and disguises is reminiscent of the end of *The Marriage of Figaro*, which serves as a model of ensemble opera for *Falstaff*.

Verdi finally cast off the traditions of Italian opera by using interweaving voices *parlando*, following the nuances of direct speech, and by handling the orchestra as chamber music. His orchestration was *predominantly light*,[183] in contrast to the contemporary tendency for vastly expanded orchestras, about which he was sometimes sarcastic. The innovative influence of this score can be seen in Puccini's *Gianni Schicchi* (1913–18), Wolf-Ferrari's *I quatro rusteghi* (*The Four Rustics, c.*1904–5), Busoni's *Die Brautwahl* (*The Bridal Choice,* 1908–11), and Richard Strauss's *Rosenkavalier* (*The Knight of the Rose,* 1909–10), and it was not just Strauss who was effusive in his praise for *Falstaff.* Ferruccio Busoni also wrote that *Falstaff* had caused 'such a revolution in his spirit and his feelings' that 'from then on he could date a chapter in his artistic life'.[184]

Richard Strauss (1864–1949) the son of a horn-player, probably contributed to the stature of that instrument more than any composer since Mozart. He took the genre of the Symphonic poem, and raised it new heights with works such as *Thus Spake Zarathustra.* In 1945 he wrote the elegaic *Metamorphosen,* lamenting the destruction of the old Germany. Bülow, acknowledging him as the 'heir' of Wagner, dubbed him 'Richard the 2nd'.

With *Falstaff* Verdi took his leave of the stage. In this final opera he made reference to many of his earlier works, often with retrospective irony: to *Un ballo in maschera* when Alice sings Oscar's harmony (Act 2, Scene 2); the servants' *Immenso Falstaff* recalls the Priestess's *Immenso Fthà* from *Aida*; the falling fifth D flat/G flat is quoted from the Chorus of Priests; and even in the judgement scene there is a play on the summons, repeated three times, each a semitone higher, by the citizens disguised as monks: *Risponde,* though here the scene is turned into a comedy, as Falstaff happily recognises Bardolph by his red nose. Ford's monologue *È sogno* is reminiscent of King Philippe's monologue in *Don Carlos.*

Above all there are many references to *Otello,* not just with the motifs for jealousy and for the kiss. Falstaff's final entrance, crowned with antlers on the first stroke of midnight, opens like

Otello's final entrance, with a 'note of terror', a *note imprévue*, while a transformed version of Otello's motif can also be heard. One of Verdi's central themes – a father's lack of control over his child, and the breaking down of authority – returns here in a comic guise. Beyond these personal reminiscences, the whole genre of traditional Italian opera is held up for a farewell scrutiny. Individual forms and traditions of opera are parodied: the 'revenge aria' in Falstaff's monologue, where he reflects on the worthlessness of honour; the 'oath scene' with its festive brass, quoted in the comic oath sworn by Dr Cajus – closing with an *Amen* from his servant, a 'false' canon in semitones; the pious women's chorus with its sanctimonious *Domine, fallo casto* picks up the tune of the Hostias from the *Requiem*, which Falstaff then parodies in his cheeky concluding remark, *salva mi l'addommine* ('preserve my paunch').

Falstaff pays homage to operas of the past in other ways too. The aria returns in Fenton's *Dal labbro il canto*, like a precious memory of earlier traditions, but the sonnet on which it is based is no longer in the first person. Here is love itself singing of its blessed position in the world – a *secret echo* in which Fenton's voice is paired with the cor anglais, and at the end with the voice of Nannetta in the distance. This is now the converse of the way in which love was portrayed in other Verdi operas, where passion finds fulfilment only in a vision at the approach of death. This perfect harmony, culminating in its top note – high B over a harp accompaniment – not used before in *Falstaff*, lasts only for a brief moment, before the masked citizens abruptly break up the duet, with a disenchantment that emphasises the quotations on which this aria is built. In the execution ritual of the finale, play is made of the fate of opera in public culture, indicating just how much autobiographical material there is in Verdi's last opera. Although he was wary of showing his feelings, he did write a sort of adieu into his copy of the manuscript: *It is all done! Go, go old John . . . Make your way for as long as you can . . . Farewell!!!!*[185]

Verdi was almost obliged to withdraw Falstaff when he discovered that Maurel, who was to take the title role, was negotiating further performances as if he owned the opera, and that he was also demanding an inordinately high fee plus a separate fee for rehearsals. Mascheroni, Faccio's successor, conducted the first performance at La Scala on 9 February 1893, before a select audience that included Puccini and Mascagni. The half hour of applause that greeted the *grand old man of Sant'Agata*[186] did not fool Verdi, who realised that *Falstaff* would never really be popular. However, its success at

In 1889 Pietro Mascagni (1863–1945) won first prize in a competition sponsored by a music publisher with his one-act opera *Cavalleria rusticana* (*Rustic Chivalry*). The success of this work overshadowed his remaining operas such as *Iris* (1897–8) and *Nerone* (*Nero*, 1934). His reputation has also suffered because of his association with Mussolini's Fascist regime.

La Scala was topped by a performance in Rome attended by King Umberto I. Verdi's 50-year career culminated in the applause he received from the royal box, and with his elevation to honorary citizen of Rome.

He was completely exhausted when he returned home from Rome. The constant thought that his life was drawing to its close paralysed him, although he could not exist without his work, of which there was still plenty. Boito took many problems off his shoulders. Although they still did

Victor Maurel (1848–1923) sang Iago and Falstaff. When he tried to make his own cuts to the part of Falstaff in Paris, Verdi exploded with rage: *And they speak of art . . . great art!! What a joke!!* [187]

not address each other as intimates, their close friendship is evident from the sympathy Verdi showed towards Boito when the latter separated, with great sadness, from Eleonora Duse, with whom he had had a relationship lasting many years. And when Boito intended to fight a duel, following an insult in Naples, Verdi waited anxiously for news, going to the railway station on several occasions until he was relieved to meet Boito there in person, the duel having been called off.

Verdi was now 80 years old, but he and Giuseppina made two journeys to Paris, for a performance of *Falstaff* at the Opéra-Comique, and of *Otello* at the Opéra. It was not only the journey that was an ordeal – there were sleeping-cars by this time – but the fact that he was continuously besieged by journalists. The Verdis received an invitation to the Élysée Palace, where the composer was decorated with the Grand Cross of the Légion d'Honneur.

Arrigo Boito and Verdi in the garden of the Ricordi publishing house in the 1880s. Giuseppina wrote of Boito's loyalty to his friends. When he admired a person, she noticed that he was 'capable of boundless enthusiasm'.[188]

He had been planning for some time to build a retirement home for impecunious musicians in Milan, a Casa di Riposo. The building work was started in 1895 under the supervision of Boito's brother, Camillo, and Verdi regularly inspected progress carrying a large umbrella to protect himself from the sun. He was still composing occasionally: three choral pieces in which he combined the very old – in Gregorian style and in that of Palestrina – with advanced compositional methods. Together with the *Ave Maria* these formed the *Quattro pezzi sacri (Four Sacred Pieces)*. Arturo Toscanini, who conducted them during the World Exhibition in Turin in 1898, took detailed advice from Verdi beforehand. Many of the younger composers sought him out, including Massenet, Mascagni, Leoncavallo, Wolf-Ferrari and Giordano, but Verdi's

Today the French composer Jules Massenet (1842–1912), is best known for his opera, *Manon,* and the *Meditation* from his opera *Thaïs,* a favourite recital piece for violinists. As a student at the Paris conservatoire, he won the 'Grand Prix' for piano at the age of 16, and later became a distinguished teacher himself, numbering Bruneau and Pierné among his students.

scepticism about contemporary music was growing. He bemoaned the preference of these *Futurists* for dissonance and endless modulations and their lack of *naturalness.*[189] He was convinced that the composers of his own country should see themselves as *heirs of Palestrina.*[190]

In January 1897 Verdi had a stroke and was unable to speak for a time. He did not want anyone to know, and merely wrote to Ricordi that he was *not feeling well.*[191] A few weeks later he was off to Milan to rehearse singers. He appeared the same as ever, and held himself 'erect' as a 'trooper'.[192]

Premières of Verismo Operas:

1889   *Edgar* by Puccini; *Gina* by Francesco Cilea (1866–1950)

1890   *Cavalleria rusticana (Rustic Chivalry)* by Pietro Mascagni (1863–1945)

1891   *L'amico Fritz (Friend Fritz)* by Mascagni

1892   *Pagliacci (Strolling Players* or *Clowns)* by Ruggero Leoncavallo (1857–1919); *Mala vita* by Umberto Giordano (1867–1948); *La Wally* by Alfredo Catalani (1854–93)

1893   *Manon Lescaut* by Puccini

1896   *La bohème (Bohemian Life)* by Puccini; *Andrea Chénier* by Giordano

1898   *Fedora* by Giordano

1900   *Tosca* by Puccini

1901   *Le maschere* by Mascagni

That summer Giuseppina was so ill she could get up only for a few hours at a time. She suffered from constant nausea, was unable to keep down food, and could hardly speak. Eventually she caught a lung infection and died on 14 November 1897. Two days later Verdi walked behind her coffin in the early morning on the long road to Villanova.

Life at Sant'Agata held no joy for him any more, so he spent longer periods in the Grand Hotel Milan, although he still paid regular visits to his estate. He slept badly, rising early and taking his coach in the mornings to inspect

Verdi seated at the table. With him, at the table, from right to left, are Teresa Stolz, Prof. Grocco, Giuseppina Pasqua, Leopoldo Mugnone and his wife.

the building works at the Casa di Riposo, which were completed only at the end of 1899. In the evenings he liked to play cards, and went to bed late so that the night would not seem so long. He was worried by the financial plight of the theatre, and in particular about the growing poverty in his own country. In 1894 he had composed the *Pietà, Signor* for the victims of the earthquake in Sicily. In the winter of 1897 the army opened fire on strikers, killing and injuring many.

Every day from my window I can see one ship, sometimes two, laden with at least 1,000 emigrants! Misery and hunger! I can see how former land-owners, as they were a few years ago, have become farmers, labourers, and exiles (misery and hunger).
Verdi to Piroli from Genoa, 10 February 1899 [193]

PIETÀ SIGNOR

Boito tried in vain to encourage Verdi to compose another opera. He was also not prepared to write his memoirs – *never, never,* he told his publisher. He would spare the music world his *prose.*[194] He was too weak to attend the first performance of his *Quattro pezzi sacri* in Paris, and besides, he said, he no longer knew anyone there. *I am not ill, but I am not particularly well; my legs will hardly support me, my eyes no longer see, my spirits are sinking, and so life is extremely hard! If only I could still work!* he complained in the spring of 1900.[195] But he had been complaining ever since he came into this world, he confessed to Ricordi in one of his last letters.[196] Filomena and her family, the Ricordis with their children, Boito, the De Amicis, and Teresa Stolz often came to visit him, and each time their visits were cause for a little period of joy. Stolz remained faithful to the end, and Verdi enjoyed her company. *Preserve your love for me,* he wrote to her six months before his death, *and believe in mine for you, which is great, very great and sincere.*[197]

In May 1900 he wrote his will. He remembered many charitable foundations: asylums, hospitals, institutions for the deaf and dumb and for the blind in Genoa, the poor of Sant'Agata, the Monte di Pietà, and the Casa di Riposo. He gave instructions that his heirs should make no changes in the house and garden at Sant'Agata. They should bury him beside Giuseppina either at dawn or in the evening to the ringing of the Ave bell but *without any singing or music.*[198]

He left Sant'Agata for the last time at the beginning of December. He celebrated Christmas, the festival which he loved the most because it reminded him of 'the sacred marvel of childhood', with his friends in Milan.[199] Then on 21 January 1901 he suffered a stroke in his hotel room. Verdi died on 27 January around 3 am. He was buried alongside Giuseppina in the cemetery in Milan on the morning of 30 January. When the two coffins were transferred to the chapel of the Casa di Riposo on 27 February, as he had

Verdi's coffin on its way to the crypt in the Casa di Riposa in Milan.

instructed in his will, more than 300,000 people turned up to bid farewell to Giuseppe Verdi, while Toscanini conducted a choir singing once again the words that had become a patriotic hymn: *Va, pensiero, sull'ali dorate* – fly, thought, on wings of gold.

Notes

Abbreviations in the notes below refer to the following titles:

A: Abbiati, Franco, *Guiseppe Verdi*, 4 volumes (Milan: 1959)
C: Cesari, Gaetano and Alessandro Luzio (ed), *I copialettere di Guiseppe Verdi* (Milan: 1913)
I: Conati, Marcello (ed), *Interviste e incontri con Verdi* (Milan: 1980)
O: Oberdorfer, Aldo (ed), *Guiseppe Verdi: autobiografia dalle lettere*, (Milan: 1951, 1981)
PM: Phillips-Matz, Mary Jane, *Verdi. A Biography*, (Oxford, New York: 1993)
VB: Medici, Mario, and Marcello Conati (ed), *Carteggio Verdi – Boito*, 2 Volumes (Parma: 1978)
W: Weaver, William (ed), *Verdi. A documentary* (Berlin: 1980)

Italian texts were translated by the author

1 PM22
2 Adolfo Rossi, *Roncole Verdi, guida storica* (Florence, 1969), p. 57ff (W141)
3 A1, 315, 245
4 Pietro Michiara (PM22)
5 A2, 152
6 C521
7 A4, 632
8 C232
9 A1, 230, 115
10 A1, 212
11 A1, 242
12 O63
13 A1, 315
14 C416
15 O62
16 *Otto Nicolais Tagebucher*, edited by Wilhelm Altmann (Regensburg, 1928), p. 211
17 O64
18 A1, 245
19 W157
20 A1, 736
21 A2, 500
22 Franz Wallner-Basté, *Verdi aus der Nahe* (Zurich, 1919), p. 79
23 Otto, *Verdi: Briefe*, p. 46
24 A1, 542
25 A1, 315
26 A1, 636
27 A2, 591
28 A1, 507
29 A1, 364
30 W163
31 A1, 507
32 A1, 466
33 PM120
34 A1, 477
35 A1, 751
36 A2, 60
37 A1, 644
38 A1, 643
39 C61
40 A1, 642.
41 A1, 673, 687
42 W168
43 A1, 712, 711
44 W169
45 A3, 335
46 A1, 711
47 A2, 275
48 A1, 745
49 A1 757
50 A1, 759
51 Frank Walker, *The Man Verdi* (London, 1962), p. 198
52 A1, 712
53 A2, 30
54 C129
55 C129
56 PM251
57 C113
58 A2, 93, 94, 137
59 C478
60 C108
61 A2, 87
62 C494
63 C497
64 Hans Busch, *Giuseppe Verdi: Briefe* (Kassel, Basel, 1979), p. 81
65 C499
66 C498
67 C539
68 C498
69 W182
70 *Bollettino dell'instituto di studi verdiani*, I, 3 (Parma, 1960), p 1765
71 C521
72 C130

73 C530
74 A2, 121
75 A2, 699
76 A2, 122
77 C532
78 A2, 189
79 Busch, *Verdi: Briefe*, p. 52
80 Azucena dreams of a happy life with a similar rocking melody at the end of *Il trovatore* (*Ai nostre monti*)
81 A2, 205, 220
82 A2, 203
83 A2, 220
84 A2, 252
85 A2, 265
86 A2, 265
87 W221
88 A2, 300
89 C443
90 A2, 375
91 VB81
92 A2, 420
93 C450
94 C478
95 A2, 368
96 A2, 459
97 C572
98 C579
99 A2, 562
100 C602
101 I62
102 A2, 673
103 A2, 762
104 A3, 64
105 A3, 129
106 I59
107 A3, 199
108 A3, 45
109 I59
110 C220
111 C521f
112 A3, 215
113 A3, 225
114 A3, 297
115 C645, 642
116 A3, 3480
117 A3, 360
118 C644

119 A3, 361
120 C687
121 W227f
122 C221, 676
123 C627
124 A4, 17
125 A3, 566
126 C280
127 A3, 749
128 A3, 518
129 A3, 508–11
130 I317
131 C302
132 Wallner-Basté, *Verdi aus der Nähe*, p. 243
133 A3, 248
134 (A3, 581)
135 Wallner-Basté, *Verdi aus der Nähe*, p. 245
136 A3, 670
137 A3, 806
138 A3, 806
139 A3, 764
140 C501
141 A3, 679
142 W230
143 W246ff
144 C291
145 Busch, *Verdi: Briefe*, p. 21
146 Werner Otto (ed), *Giuseppe Verdi: Briefe* (Kassel, Basel, 1983), p. 243
147 C524, 523
148 A4, 26
149 From the report by De Amicis, in Busch, *Briefwechsel Verdi–Boito*, p. 597
150 A4, 96
151 A4, 123
152 PM665, 684
153 I153, 156, 155
154 Hans Busch (ed), *Verdi–Boito Briefwechsel* (Frankfurt, 1986), p. 45
155 Hans Busch (ed), *Verdi–Boito Briefwechsel* (Frankfurt, 1986), p. 63

156 A4, 203
157 A4, 232
158 C630
159 C631
160 Busch, *Verdi: Briefe*, p. 170
161 C629ff
162 A4, 203
163 C503
164 VB78
165 C322
166 C344
167 C526
168 C700
169 A4, 352
170 W243
171 VB57
172 A4, 337
173 A4, 434
174 A4, 329
175 VB146
176 C711
177 I223
178 VB179
179 Busch, *Briefwechsel Verdi–Boito*, p. 591
180 C528
181 C505
182 VB207
183 A4, 519
184 Reinhard Erman, *Ferruccio Busoni* (Reinbek, 1996), p. 49
185 Busch, *Verdi–Boito*, p. 352
186 C713
187 A4, 544
188 A4, 113
189 VB224ff
190 C702
191 A4, 604
192 I284
193 A4, 360
194 C403
195 O106
196 A4, 651
197 A4,657
198 A4, 656
199 Busch, *Verdi–Boito*, p. 517

Glossary of Musical Terms

a cappella   Unaccompanied choral singing ('in the chapel style').

adagio   A slow movement or piece.

agitato   'Agitated', in an agitated manner.

allegretto   Not quite so fast as *allegro*.

allegro   'Fast', but not too fast.

allegro moderato 'Moderately fast'.

andante   At a walking pace, not so slow as *adagio* nor as fast as *allegretto*.

andantino   A little quicker than *andante*.

aria   A lengthy and well-developed solo vocal piece in ABA form (ie in three sections, the third part being a repeat of the first). The singer is expected to add ornaments in the repeated A section.

arioso   In the style of an *aria*; halfway between *aria* and *recitative*.

arpeggio   Notes of a chord played in a broken, spread-out manner, as on a harp.

bacchanale   An orgiastic composition (from the Latin *bacchanalia*: a feast of dancing and singing in honour of Bacchus, the Greek or Roman god of wine).

barcarole   A boating-song, reminiscent of songs of the Venetian gondoliers or barcaruoli.

bel canto   'Beautiful singing' in the old Italian style with pure tone and exact phrasing.

buffo(a)   'Comic', as in *opera buffa*.

cabaletta   The final quick section of an *aria* or *duet*.

cadenza   A virtuosic passage for a solo instrument or voice, usually near the close of a movement of a concerto, sometimes improvised.

cantabile   'Song-like, singable'; a lyrical 'singing' style, flowing and expressive.

cantata   Vocal work for chorus and/or choir.

cantilena	'Cradle song': vocal writing that is smooth, sustained, melodious, and not too fast.
cantus firmus	'Fixed song'. A basic melody, usually taken from *plainsong*, used by composers from the fourteenth to the seventeenth century, around which other voices weave *contrapuntal* parts.
cavatina	An operatic solo *aria* in one section; or a slow, song-like instrumental movement.
chorus	A substantial body of singers, usually singing in four parts; *mixed voice* (men and women) or *male voice* (boys and men).
chromatic	Using the chromatic scale of twelve ascending or descending semitones (sharps ascending, flats descending); from the Greek *chromos*: colour.
colla voce	'With the voice'. An indication to the accompanist to take his tempos and rhythm from the soloist.
coloratura	The elaborate and agile ornamentation of a melody with runs, cadenzas, trills, roulades, etc.
concertato	Writing for several solo instruments to be played together.
contrapuntal	The adjective of *counterpoint*.
counterpoint	Simultaneous combination of two or more melodies to create a satisfying musical texture; one melody is the counterpoint of the other. From the expression *punctus contra punctum*: note against note.
credo	'I believe'. Section of the Mass frequently set by composers, but in opera the statement of a belief by a character (see Iago's aria in Act 2 of *Otello* in which he states his belief in a cruel God).
divisi	'Divided', as when orchestral string parts are written in double (or more) notes and the players divide themselves into two (or more) groups to perform them.
ensemble	Literally 'together': a group of performers of no fixed number; an item in opera for several singers with or without chorus.
falsetto	A singing method used by male tenors to achieve higher notes beyond the normal range of their voice. Often used for comic effect.
fugue	Contrapuntal composition for a particular number of parts or voices. The parts or voices enter successively in imitation of each other.

galop or *galopade*	A nineteenth-century ballroom round dance in a simple dupal time, with a change of step or hop at the end of every musical phrase.
glissando	Rapid sliding scales up and down piano or other instruments.
harmony	The simultaneous sounding of notes so as to make musical sense.
interval	The distance between two notes.
inversion	The turning upside down of a chord, interval, counterpoint, theme, or pedal point.
largo	Slow, broad, dignified in style.
legato	'Bound together'. In a smooth style, the opposite of *staccato*.
leggiero	'Light'.
major	One of two main scales of the tonal system with semitones between the third and fourth, and the seventh and eighth notes.
marcato	'Marked, marking', with each note emphasised.
mazurka	A traditional Polish country dance, not fast but dignified and with a touch of abandon.
mediant	The third degree of the major or minor scale, midway between the tonic and the dominant.
melisma	A group of notes sung to a single syllable (from the Greek for 'song'), as opposed to *coloratura*.
minor	The opposite of *major*, as applied to a scale, key, chord, or intervals.
minuet	A dance in triple time with many dainty steps.
modulation	Changing from key to key in a composition according to the evolution of musical 'grammar' (ie not by stopping and starting in a new key).
motif	A short, easily recognised melodic figure.
obbligato	'Indispensable'. An obligatory, special, or unusual instrumental part in a piece.
opera buffa	Comic opera usually involving characters drawn from everyday life in contrast to the mythical subjects of *opera seria* (serious opera).

ostinato	'Obstinate, insistent'. A persistently repeated musical phrase or rhythm.
parlando	'Speaking'. In vocal music indicating a tone of voice, and in instrumental music calling for an expressive, conversational freedom.
piano	Soft, quiet; pianissimo meaning very soft and quiet.
plainsong	Medieval church music consisting of a single line of vocal melody without harmony or definite rhythm.
postlude	A piece played at the end. The opposite of a prelude.
presto	'Quick, very fast'.
rataplan	A drumming sound, imitative of a drum.
recitative	A form of declamatory speech-like singing used in opera dialogue or narrative to advance the plot. Less static or reflective than an *aria*.
ritornello	A refrain or recurring passage in a piece, usually instrumental.
rococo	In a decorative style, no longer baroque but not yet classical.
romance	Generally a piece of a personal or tender song-like character.
roulade	A French vocal ornament.
saraband	A dance form originating in Spain. Sarabands became a standard movement of the suite in instrumental works by Purcell, J S Bach, and Handel.
scala enigmatica	Literally 'enigmatic scale', a term applied to the arbitrary scale used by Verdi in his *Ave Maria* (1897), the first of his *Quattro pezzi sacri*.
scena	Literally 'scene'. An elaborate concert *aria* for voice and orchestra in several sections.
scherzando	In a playful manner.
scherzo	'Joke'. The third (or sometimes second) movement of a symphony or string quartet, etc; the liveliest movement but not necessarily light-hearted.
semitone	Half a tone. The smallest interval in European music.
sequence	The more or less exact repetition of a passage at a higher or lower level of pitch.
siciliano(a)	'Sicilian'. A type of dance, song, or instrumental piece presumably of Sicilian origin, in compound duple or

quadruple time and with a swaying rhythm often in a minor key.

sotto voce   'Below the voice'. In an undertone or barely audible (like an aside).

staccato   'Detached'. A method of playing a note so that it is shortened ('detached' from its successor) by being held for less than its full value.

stretta   'Drawn together'. The passage at the end of an Italian operatic aria, ensemble, or act where the tempo is quickened for the final climax.

stretto   'Drawn together'. A quicker tempo.

syncopation   A device used by composers in order to vary the position of the stress on notes so as to avoid regular rhythm. Exploited to its fullest capabilities in jazz.

tremolo   'Shaking, trembling'. In playing a stringed instrument, the rapid reiteration of a note or chord by back-and-forth strokes of the bow.

trill   An ornament comprising rapid alternation of the main note and the note above, normally slurred and associated with cadences.

tutti   'Everybody'. A passage in which the orchestra plays without the soloist.

vivacissimo   Very fast.

GLOSSARY OF MUSICAL TERMS

Chronology

Year	Age	Life
1813		10 October: Giuseppe Verdi born in Le Roncole.
1817	4	Begins lessons with Pietro Baistrocchi.
1822	9	Becomes the organist at the church in Le Roncole.
1823	10	Goes to school in Busseto.
1831	18	Taken in by the Barezzis.
1832	19	Fails the entrance exams for the Milan Conservatory. Private lessons from Vincenzo Lavigna.
1836	23	Appointed *maestro di musica* in Busseto. Marries Margherita Barezzi. Writes first opera *Rocester* (now lost).
1837	24	Daughter Virginia born.
1838	25	Son Icilio born. Virginia dies. Abandons his position in Busseto.

Year	History	Culture
1813	Battle of Leipzig. Mexico declares itself independent. In Venezuela, Simón Bolívar becomes dictator. Persia cedes Caucasus region to Russia.	Gioacchino Rossini, *Tancredi* and *The Italian Girl in Algiers*. Jane Austen, *Pride and Prejudice*. Lord Byron, *Childe Harold's Pilgrimage*.
1817	In Britain, *Habeas corpus* suspended. In US, James Monroe becomes president. In India, the third Maratha War (until 1818).	Georg Hegel, *Encyclopaedia of the Philosophical sciences*. David Ricardo, *Principles of Political Economy*.
1822	In Africa, Liberia founded for freed US slaves. Congress of Verona. Greece declares independence. Brazil declares independence.	
1823	Monroe Doctrine: excludes European powers from interfering in politics of American republics. Mexico becomes republic. First Anglo-Burmese War.	
1831	In Belgium, Leopold of Saxe-Coburg becomes king of independent state. In India, English East India Company annexes Mysore. In Brazil, Pedro I abdicates. Charles Darwin begins voyage on the Beagle.	Vincenzo Bellini, *Norma*. Victor Hugo, *Notre-Dame de Paris*. Eugène Delacroix, *La Liberté guidant le peuple*.
1832	Britain proclaims sovereignty over Falkland Islands. Turkish-Egyptian War (until 1833). In continental Europe, first railway. In US, Black Hawk War.	Gaetano Donizetti, *L'Elisir d'Amore*. Alexander Pushkin, *Eugene Onegin*. Johann Wolfgang von Goethe, *Faust* (part II).
1836	Texas becomes independent of Mexico. In south Africa, Great Trek of Boers.	R W Emerson's *Nature* founds Transcendentalism.
1837	In Britain, William IV dies; Victoria becomes queen (until 1901). In US, Martin van Buren becomes president. In Canada, rebellions in Upper and Lower Canada (until 1838).	Charles Dickens, *Pickwick Papers*.
1838	In Britain, People's Charter initiates Chartist movement. In South Africa, Battle of Blood River. First Anglo-Afghan War (until 1842). Steamship service established between Britain and the US.	In London, National Gallery opens.

Year	Age	Life
1839	26	Moves to Milan. Icilio dies. Première of *Oberto*.
1840	27	Margherita dies. Première of *Un giorno di regno*.
1841	28	Starts work on *Nabucco*. Meets Giuseppina Strepponi.
1842	29	Première of *Nabucco*.
1843	30	Première of *I Lombardi alla prima crociata*.
1844	31	Premières of *Ernani* and *I due Foscari*.
1845	32	Premières of *Giovanna d'Arco* and *Alzira*. Break-up of relations with La Scala. Buys the Palazzo Cavalli in Busseto.
1846	33	Première of *Attila*.
1847	34	Première of *Macbeth*. Travels to London (première of *I masnadieri*) and Paris (première of *Jérusalem*).
1848	35	Buys an estate in Sant'Agata. Première of *Il corsaro*. Travels to Paris and Rome.
1849	36	Première of *La battaglia di Legnano*. Moves into the Palazzo Cavalli with Giuseppina Strepponi. Première of *Luisa Miller*.
1850	37	Première of *Stiffelio*.

Year	History	Culture
1839	Britain acquires Aden. Britain proclaims New Zealand a colony. Turkish-Egyptian War: Egypt loses Syria (until 1841). First Opium War (until 1842).	Dickens, *Nicholas Nickelby*. Edgar Allan Poe, *Tales of the Grotesque and Arabesque*. J M W Turner, *Fighting Téméraire*.
1840	In New Zealand, Treaty of Waitangi: Maori chiefs surrender sovereignty to Britain. In Canada, Act of Union joins Lower and Upper Canada.	Robert Schumann, *Dichterliebe*. Adolphe Sax invents the saxophone. P J Proudhon, *Qu'est-ce-que la Propriété?*
1841	In east Africa, Said ibn Sayyid makes Zanzibar his capital. Egypt declares independence from Turkey. Second Anglo-Afghan War.	In Britain, *Punch* magazine founded.
1842	France occupies Tahiti, Guinea and Gabon. In North America, border established between Canada and US. Treaty of Nanjing: Britain acquires Hong Kong.	Richard Wagner, *Rienzi*. Nikolai Gogol, *Dead Souls*. Alfred Lord Tennyson, *Morte D'Arthur and Other Idylls*.
1843	In India, Britain annexes Sind. In south Africa, Britain proclaims Natal a colony.	Wagner, *Flying Dutchman*. John Stuart Mill, *Logic*.
1844	In Morocco, war with France.	Dumas, *The Count of Monte Cristo*.
1845	In Ireland, potato famine. In India, Anglo-Sikh War (until 1848–9).	Benjamin Disraeli, *Sybil*.
1846	Mexico-US War (until 1848). In southern Africa, second Xhosa War. In Asia, Britain acquires Labuan, Malaya.	Hector Berlioz, *The Damnation of Faust*. Felix Mendelssohn, *Elijah*. Edward Lear, *Book of Nonsense*.
1847	In Yucután Peninsula, War of the Castes. In France, reform banquets held. In Switzerland, Sonderbund War. In California, gold rush begins.	Charlotte Brontë, *Jane Eyre*. Emily Brontë, *Wuthering Heights*.
1848	In continental Europe, revolutions in: Sicily; Naples; Paris; Vienna; Venice; Milan; Warsaw; and Cracow. In France, Second Republic begins (until 1851). In India, second Sikh War (until 1849). In French West Indies, slavery abolished.	William Thackeray, *Vanity Fair*. Engels and Karl Marx, *The Communist Manifesto*. H Holman Hunt, J Millais and D G Rossetti form the Pre-Raphaelite Brotherhood.
1849	In Rome, republic proclaimed; French troops take Rome. In India, Britain annexes Punjab.	Dickens, *David Copperfield*.
1850	In Rome, Pope Pius IX restored. In Britain, re-establishment of Roman Catholic hierarchy. In China, Taping Rebellion (until 1864). Robert Wilhelm von Bunsen invents Bunsen burner. J W Brett lays first submarine cable, between Dover and Calais.	Nathanial Hawthorne, *The Scarlet Letter*. Lord Tennyson, *In Memoriam*. Millais, *Christ in the House of his Parents*.

Year	Age	Life
1851	38	Première of *Rigoletto*. Moves into Sant'Agata. Mother dies. Journey to Paris.
1853	40	Premières of *Il trovatore* and *La traviata*. Travels to Paris.
1855	42	Première of *Les vêpres siciliennes* at the Paris Opéra.
1857	44	Premières of *Simon Boccanegra* and *Aroldo*.
1859	46	Première of *Un ballo in maschera*. Marries Giuseppina Strepponi.
1861	48	Elected to Parliament. Starts work on *La forza del destino* and travels to Russia.
1862	49	Second journey to Russia for the première of *La forza del destino*.
1863	50	Travels to Spain and Paris.
1865	52	Première of a revised version of *Macbeth* in Paris. Resigns his seat in Parliament.
1866	53	Rents the Palazzo Sauli in Genoa. Travels to Paris. Finishes work on *Don Carlos*.
1867	54	Première of *Don Carlos*. Father dies. Adopts Filomena. Death of Barezzi.

Year	History	Culture
1851	In France, Louis Napoleon leads *coup d'état*. Isaac Singer invents sewing machine.	Herman Melville, *Moby Dick*.
1852	France annexes New Caledonia. Russia conquers Kazakhstan. In Crimea, fighting between Russia and Turkey. In China, Nien Rebellion (until 1868). In India, first railways and telegraph.	
1855	In Russia, Nicholas I dies; Alexander II becomes tsar (until 1881). In southern Africa, D Livingstone 'discovers' Victoria Falls.	Robert Browning, *Men and Women*. Gaskell, *North and South*. Walt Whitman, *Leaves of Grass*.
1857	In India, mutiny against British (until 1858). In Africa, J H Speke 'discovers' source of the Nile. Laying of cable under Atlantic Ocean begun (until 1865).	Charles Baudelaire, *Les Fleurs du Mal*. Gustave Flaubert, *Madame Bovary*. Anthony Trollope, *Barchester Towers*.
1859	Franco-Piedmontese War against Austria. Spanish-Moroccan War (until 1860). Construction of Suez Canal begins (until 1869).	Wagner, *Tristan und Isolde*. Edward Fitzgerald, *Rubaiyat of Omar Khayyam*. Charles Darwin, *The Origin of Species*.
1861	In US, Abraham Lincoln becomes president (until 1865). In US, Civil War begins (until 1865). In Italy, Victor Emmanuel II becomes king. In Russia, serfdom abolished. In Britain, death of Prince Albert.	Dickens, *Great Expectations*. Eliot, *Silas Marner*. In Britain, William Morris begins to make wallpapers and tapestries.
1862	In Prussia, Otto von Bismarck becomes premier.	Hugo, *Les Misérables*. Turgenev, *Fathers and Sons*.
1863	In US, slavery abolished. In Asia, Cambodia becomes French protectorate. Polish uprising against Russia.	Berlioz, *The Trojans* (part I). Charles Kingsley, *The Water Babies*. Manet, *Déjeuner sur l'herbe*.
1865	In US, Abraham Lincoln assassinated. In South America, Paraguayan war (until 1870). End of transport of convicts to Australia.	Lewis Carroll, *Alice's Adventures in Wonderland*.
1866	Austro-Prussian War. Austro-Italian War. In Canada, Fenian 'invasion'. Alfred Nobel invents dynamite. Gregor Mendel develops laws of heredity.	Friedrich Smetana, *The Bartered Bride*. Fyodor Dostoevsky, *Crime and Punishment*.
1867	Prussia forms North German Confederation. Austria forms Austro-Hungarian empire. US purchases Alaska from Russia. British North America Act creates Dominion of Canada. Joseph Lister introduces antiseptic surgery.	Joseph Strauss, *The Blue Danube*. Marx, *Das Kapital*. Henrik Ibsen, *Peer Gynt*.

Year	Age	Life
1868	55	Meets Alessandro Manzoni. Death of Rossini.
1870	57	Journey to Paris. Composes *Aida*.
1871	58	*Lohengrin* is given in Bologna. *Aida* premières in Cairo.
1873	60	Composes the String Quartet in E minor.
1874	61	The *Requiem* is performed on the anniversary of the death of Alessandro Manzoni. Verdi moves from the Palazzo Sauli into the Palazzo Doria. Appointed a senator.
1878	65	Filomena Verdi marries Alberto Carrara.
1879	66	Boito finishes work on the libretto of *Otello*.
1880	67	Travels to Paris for performances of *Aida* in French.
1881	68	Première of the new version of *Simon Boccanegra*.
1883	70	Death of Richard Wagner.

Year	History	Culture
1868	In Britain, William Gladstone becomes prime minister (until 1874). In Japan, Meiji dynasty restored. In Britain, Trades' Union Congress founded.	Johannes Brahms, *A German Requiem*. W Collins, *The Moonstone*. Dostoevsky, *The Idiot*.
1870	Franco-Prussian War. Papal Rome annexed by Italy. In US, John Rockefeller founds Standard Oil.	Clément Delibes, *Coppélia*. Dostoevsky, *The House of the Dead*.
1871	At Versailles, William I proclaimed German emperor. In France, Third Republic suppresses Paris Commune and loses Alsace-Lorraine to Germany. In Germany, *Kulturkampf* begins.	Caroll, *Through the Looking-Glass*.
1873	In Spain, Amadeo I abdicates; republic proclaimed. In Africa, Ashanti War begins (until 1874). In Asia, Acheh War (until 1903). Great Depression (until 1896).	Arthur Rimbaud, *A Season in Hell*. Walter Pater, *Studies in the History of the Renaissance*. Claude Monet, *Impression: soleil levant*.
1874	In Britain, Benjamin Disraeli becomes prime minister. In Spain, Alfonso XII establishes constitutional monarchy. Britain annexes Fiji islands.	Smetana, *My Fatherland*. J Strauss, *Die Fledermaus*. In Paris, first Impressionist exhibition.
1878	Congress of Berlin resolves Balkan crisis. Serbia becomes independent. Britain gains Cyprus. Second Anglo-Afghan War (until 1879). In London, electric street lighting.	Tchaikovsky, *Swan Lake*.
1879	Germany and Austria-Hungary form Dual Alliance. In Africa, Zulu War. In south Africa, Boers proclaim Transvaal Republic. In South America, War of the Pacific (until 1883).	Anton Bruckner, Sixth Symphony. Tchaikovsky, *Eugene Onegin*. Ibsen, *The Doll's House*. August Strindberg, *The Red Room*.
1880	In Britain, William Gladstone becomes prime minister. First Boer War (until 1881). Louis Pasteur discovers streptococcus.	Tchaikovsky, *1812 Overture*. Dostoevsky, *The Brothers Karamazov*.
1881	In Russia, Alexander II assassinated. In Japan, political parties established. Tunisia becomes French protectorate. In Algeria, revolt against the French. In Sudan, Mahdi Holy War (until 1898). In eastern Europe, Jewish pogroms.	Jacques Offenbach, *The Tales of Hoffmann*. Anatole France, *Le Crime de Sylvestre Bonnard*. Henry James, *Portrait of Lady*. Ibsen, *Ghosts*.
1883	Jewish immigration to Palestine (Rothschild Colonies). Germany acquires southwest Africa. In Chicago, world's first skyscraper built.	Antonín Dvorák, *Stabat Mater*. Robert Louis Stevenson, *Treasure Island*.

Year	Age	Life
1884	71	Première of *Don Carlos* (four-act version).
1886	73	Death of Clara Maffei. Finishes *Otello*.
1887	74	Première of *Otello*.
1888	75	Opens the hospital in Villanova.
1890	77	Death of Emanuele Muzio.
1893	80	Première of *Falstaff*. Verdi is decorated by Umberto I in Rome.
1894	81	Travels to Paris twice for performances of *Otello* and *Falstaff*.
1895	82	Negotiations about the retirement home for musicians (Casa di Riposo) and building work begins. Starts work on his *Te Deum*.
1897	84	Suffers a stroke. Continues work on the *Quattro pezzi sacri*. 14 November: Giuseppina dies.
1900	87	The Casa di Riposo opens. Verdi makes his will.
1901		27 January: Verdi dies. 30 January: Verdi's funeral in Milan. Husband and wife are buried in the chapel of the Casa di Riposo.

Year	History	Culture
1884	Sino-French War (until 1885). Berlin Conference to mediate European claims in Africa (until 1885). In Mexico, Porfirio Diaz becomes president (until 1911).	Jules Massenet, *Manon*. Mark Twain, *Huckleberry Finn*. Georges Seurat, *Une Baignade, Asnières*.
1886	In Cuba, slavery abolished. In India, first meeting of National Congress. In Canada, Canadian Pacific Railway completed.	Stevenson, *Dr Jekyll and Mr Hyde*. Rimbaud, *Les Illuminations*. Leo Tolstoy, *The Death of Ivan Ilich*.
1887	In Britain, Queen Victoria celebrates Golden Jubilee. Reinsurance Treaty between Germany and Russia. Heinrich Hertz produces radio waves.	
1888	In Germany, William II becomes emperor (until 1918). In Asia, French Indo-China established. In Brazil, slavery abolished.	N Rimsky-Korsakov, *Scheherezade* (op 35). Edward Bellamy, *Looking Backwards*. Rudyard Kipling, *Plain Tales from the Hills*.
1890	In Germany, Otto von Bismarck dismissed. In Spain, universal suffrage.	Tchaikovsky, *The Queen of Spades*. Ibsen, *Hedda Gabler*.
1893	Franco-Russian alliance signed. South Africa Company launches Matabele War. France annexes Laos.	Dvorák, *From the New World*. Oscar Wilde, *A Woman of No Importance*.
1894	In France, President Carnot assassinated. Alfred Dreyfus convicted of treason. In Russia, Nicholas II becomes tsar (until 1917). Sino-Japanese War (until 1895). In US, Pullman strike.	Claude Debussy, *L'Après-midi d'un Faune*. Gabriele d'Annuzio, *Il trionfo della morte*. Kipling, *The Jungle Book*. G B Shaw, *Arms and Man*.
1895	In Britain, Lord Salisbury becomes prime minister. Cuban rebellion begins. Japan conquers Taiwan (Formosa). Lumière brothers invent the cinematograph. Guglielmo Marconi invents wireless telegraphy. Wilhelm Röntgen invents X-rays.	H G Wells, *The Time Machine*. W B Yeats, *Poems*. Wilde, *The Importance of Being Earnest*.
1897	In Britain, Queen Victoria celebrates Diamond Jubilee. Britain destroys Benin City. Klondike gold rush (until 1899). J J Thomson discovers electron.	Stefan George, *Das Jahr der Seele*. Strindberg, *Inferno*. Edmond Rostand, *Cyrano de Bergerac*.
1900	Second Boer War (until 1902).First Pan-African Conference. In France, Dreyfus pardoned. Relief of Mafeking. In China, Boxer Rebellion (until 1901).	Berlioz, *The Taking of Troy*. Edward Elgar, *Enigma Variations*. George, *Der Teppich des Lebens*.
1901	In Britain, Victoria dies; Edward VII becomes king. In US, William McKinley assassinated; Theodore Roosevelt becomes president.	Giacomo Puccini, *Tosca*. Conrad, *Lord Jim*. Sigmund Freud, *The Interpretation of Dreams*.

List of Works

Operas

Oberto, Conte di San Bonifacio. Opera in two acts. Libretto: Piazza, revised by Solera. Milan, La Scala, 17 November 1839.

Un giorno di regno (originally *Il finto Stanislao*). Comic opera in two acts. Libretto: Romani. Milan, La Scala, 5 September 1840.

Nabucco. Opera in four acts. Libretto: Solera. Milan, La Scala, 9 March 1842.

I Lombardi alla prima crociata. Opera in four acts. Libretto: Solera. Milan, La Scala, 11 February 1843.

Ernani. Opera in four acts. Libretto: Piave (after a play by Victor Hugo). Venice, La Fenice, 9 March 1844.

I due Foscari. Opera in three acts. Libretto: Piave (after a drama by Lord Byron). Rome, Argentina, 3 November 1844.

Giovanna d'Arco. Opera in prologue and three acts. Libretto: Solera (after a play by Friedrich Schiller). Milan, La Scala, 15 February 1845.

Alzira. Opera in prologue and two acts. Libretto: Cammarano (after play by Voltaire). Naples, San Carlo, 12 August 1845.

Attila. Opera in prologue and three acts. Libretto: Solera (after Zacharias Werner). Venice, La Fenice, 17 March 1846.

Macbeth. Opera in four acts. Libretto: Piave and Maffei (after a play by William Shakespeare). Florence, Pergola, 14 March 1847. New version: Paris, Théâtre Lyrique, 21 April 1865.

I masnadieri. Opera in four acts. Libretto: Maffei (after a play by Friedrich Schiller). London, Her Majesty's, 22 July 1847.

Jérusalem (reworking of *I Lombardi*). Opera in four acts. Libretto: Royer and Vaëz. Paris, Opéra, 26 November 1847.

Il corsaro. Opera in three acts. Libretto: Piave (after a poem by Lord Byron). Trieste, Teatro Grande, 25 October 1848.

La battaglia di Legnano. Opera in three acts. Libretto: Cammarano (after drama by Joseph Méry). Rome, Argentina, 27 January 1849.

Luisa Miller. Opera in three acts. Libretto: Cammarano (after a play by Friedrich Schiller). Naples, San Carlo, 8 December 1849.

Stiffelio. Opera in three acts. Libretto: Piave (after a play by Emille Souvestre and Eugène Bourgeois). Trieste, Teatro Grande, 16 November 1850.

Rigoletto. Opera in three acts. Libretto: Piave (after a play by Victor Hugo). Venice, La Fenice, 11 March 1851.

Il trovatore. Opera in four acts. Libretto: Cammarano and Bardare (after a play by Antonio García y Gutiérrez). Rome, Apollo, 19 January 1851.

La traviata. Opera in three acts. Libretto: Piave (after a play by Alexandre Dumas *fils*) Venice, La Fenice, 6 March 1853.

Les vêpres siciliennes. Opera in five acts. Libretto: Scribe and Duveyrier. Paris, Opéra, 13 June 1855.

Simon Boccanegra. Opera in prologue and three acts. Libretto: Piave and Montanelli (after a play by Antonio García Gutiérrez). Venice, La Fenice, 12 March 1857. New version by Arrigo Boito. Milan, La Scala, 24 March 1881.

Aroldo (new version of *Stiffelio*). Opera in four acts. Libretto: Piave. Rimini, Teatro Nuovo, 16 August 1857.

Un ballo in maschera. Opera in three acts. Libretto: Somma (after a libretto by Eugène Scribe). Rome, Apollo, 17 February 1859.

La forza del destino. Opera in four acts. Libretto: Piave (after drama by Ángel Saavedra). St Petersburg, Imperial Theatre, 10 November 1862.

Don Carlos. Opera in five acts. Libretto: Méry and Du Locle (after a play by Friedrich Schiller). Paris, Opéra, 11 March 1867. Italian version: *Don Carlo.* Opera in four acts. Milan, Scala, 10 January 1884.

Aida. Opera in four acts. Libretto: Ghislanzoni (based on a plot by Auguste Mariette Bêy). Cairo, Opera House, 24 December 1871.

Otello. Opera in four acts. Libretto: Boito (after a play by William Shakespeare). Milan, La Scala, 5 February 1887.

Falstaff. Comic opera in three acts. Libretto: Boito (after William Shakespeare). Milan, La Scala, 9 February 1893.

Religious Works

Tantum ergo for tenor and organ, 1835.

Libera me for soprano, choir, and orchestra, 1862 (part of a *Requiem* for Rossini).

Messa da Requiem for four soloists, choir, and orchestra, 1874 (in memory of the anniversary of the death of Alessandro Manzoni).

Pater noster for a five-part choir a cappella, 1879.

Ave Maria for soprano and string orchestra, 1880.

Quattro pezzi sacri:
1 *Ave Maria* for a four-part choir a cappella, 1889.
2 *Stabat Mater* for choir and orchestra, 1898.
3 *Laudi alla Vergine Maria* for a four-part female choir a cappella, 1898.
4 *Te Deum* for a double choir and orchestra (1895).

Pietà, Signor! for tenor and piano, 1894 (to benefit the victims of the earthquake in Sicily and Calabria).

Other

Six Romances for solo voice and piano, 1838.

L'esule (The Exile); *La seduzione* (The Seduction); *Notturno: Guarda che bianca luna* (Nocturne: See the Pale Moon). Songs, 1839.

Chi i bei di m'adduce ancora (Who Will Bring Back the Beautiful Days?). Song, 1842.

Six Romances, 1845.

Il poveretto (The Beggar). Song, 1847.

Suona la tromba (Sound the Trumpet). Hymn for male choir, 1848.

L'Abandonée (The Forsaken Woman). Song, 1849.

Fiorellin che sorge appena (The Little Flower that Rises). Song, 1850.

La preghiera del poeta (The Poet's Prayer). Song, 1858.

Il brigidin (The Rosette). Song, 1863.

Tu dici che non m'ami (You Say You Do Not Love Me). Song, 1869.

String quartet in E minor, 1873.

Select Discography

String Quartet in E min. CRD CRD 3366. Alberni Qt – DONIZETTI: Quartet No. 13; PUCCINI: Crisantemi.

Requiem Mass; (ii) 4 Sacred Pieces. EMI CMS5 67560-2 [567563]. (i) Schwarzkopf, Ludwig, Gedda, Ghiaurov; (ii) J. Baker; Philh. Ch. & O, Giulini.

Aida (complete). EMI mono CDS5 56316-2 (3). Callas, Tucker, Barbieri, Gobbi, La Scala, Milan, Ch. & O, Serafin.

Un ballo in maschera (complete). DG Double 453 148-2 (2). Ricciarelli, Domingo, Bruson, Obraztsova, Gruberová, Raimondi, La Scala, Milan, Ch. & O, Abbado.

Don Carlos (complete). Ph. 454 463-2 (3). Gorchakova, Borodina, Hvorostovsky, Margison, Scandiuzzi, ROHCG Ch. & O, Haitink.

Ernani (complete). Decca 421 412-2 (2). Pavarotti, Sutherland, Nucci, Burchuladze, Welsh Nat. Op. Ch. & O, Bonynge.

Falstaff (complete). EMI CDS5 67083-2 (2). Gobbi, Schwarzkopf, Zaccaria, Moffo, Panerai, Philh. Ch. & O, Karajan.

La forza del destino (complete). RCA (ADD) 74321 39502-2 (3). L. Price, Domingo, Milnes, Cossotto, Giaiotti, Bacquier, Alldis Ch., LSO, Levine.

I Lombardi (complete). Decca 455 287-2 (2). Pavarotti, Anderson, Leech, Ramey, Met. Opera Ch. & O, Levine.

Macbeth (complete). Ph. 412 133-2 (3). Bruson, Zampieri, Shicoff, Lloyd, German Op. Ch. & O, Berlin, Sinopoli.

Nabucco (complete). Decca (ADD) 417 407-2 (2). Gobbi, Suliotis, Cava, Previdi, V. State Op. Ch. & O. Gardelli.

Otello (complete). EMI mono CHS5 65751-2 (2). Vinay, Martinis, Schöffler, Dermota, V. State Op. Ch., VPO, Furtwängler.

Rigoletto (complete). DG (ADD) 457 753-2 (2). Cappuccilli, Cotrubas, Domingo, Obraztsova, Ghiaurov, Moll, Schwarz, V. State Op. Ch., VPO, Giulini.

Simon Boccanegra (complete). DG (ADD) 449 752-2 (2). Freni, Cappuccilli, Ghiaurov, Van Dam, Carreras, La Scala, Milan, Ch. & O, Abbado.

La traviata (complete). Double Decca 443 002-2 (2). Lorengar, Aragall, Fischer-Dieskau, Ch. & O of German Op., Berlin, Maazel.

Il trovatore (complete). RCA (ADD) 74321 39504-2 (2). L. Price, Domingo, Milnes, Cossotto, Amb. Op. Ch., New Philh. O, Mehta.

Further Reading

Abbiati, Franco, *Guiseppe Verdi*, 4 volumes (Milan: 1959).

Amis, John and Rose, Michael, *Words About Music* (London: 1989).

Anderson, James, *Dictionary of Opera and Operetta* (Columbia Marketing: 1989).

Beecham, Sir Thomas, *A Mingled Chime* (London: 1944).

Bonavia, Ferruccio, *Verdi* (Oxford: 1930).

Budden, Julian, *Verdi* (London: 1985).

Budden, Julian, *The Operas of Verdi* (Oxford: 1992).

Cesari, Gaetano and Alessandro Luzio (ed), *I copialettere di Guiseppe Verdi* (Milan: 1913).

Conari, Marcello & Medici, Mario, *The Verdi-Boito Correspondence* (Chicago/London: 1994).

Dent, Edward J, *Opera: The Musical Companion* (ed. A L Bacharach), (London: 1934).

Dent, Edward J, *Opera* (London: 1940).

Douglas, Nigel, *Legendary Voices* (London: 1992).

Douglas, Nigel, *More Legendary Voices* (London: 1994).

Gatti, Carlo, *Verdi*, 2 Volumes (Milan: 1931, 1951).

Gerigk, Herbert, *Giuseppe Verdi* (Potsdam: 1932).

Gobbi, Tito, *World of Italian Opera* (London: 1984).

Headington, Christopher; Westbrook, Roy; Barfoot, Terry, *Opera – A History* (London: 1987).

Hopkins, Antony, *Music All Around Me* (London: 1967).

Hussey, Dyneley, *Verdi* (London: 1948).

Lebrecht, Norman, *The Book of Musical Anecdotes* (London: 1985).

Marggraf, Wolfgang, *Giuseppe Verdi. Life and Work* (Leipzig: 1982)

Martin, George, *Aspects of Verdi* (London: 1988).

Matthews, Denis, *In Pursuit of Music* (London: 1966).

Matthews, Denis, *Arturo Toscanini* (Tunbridge Wells: 1982).

Oberdorfer, Aldo (ed), *Guiseppe Verdi: autobiografia dalle lettere* (Milan: 1951, 1981).

Osborne, Charles, *The Complete Operas of Verdi* (London: 1988).

Osborne, Charles, *Letters of Giuseppe Verdi* (London: 1971).

Osborne, Charles, *Verdi* (London: 1978).

Parker, Roger (ed), *The Oxford Illustrated History of Opera* (Oxford: 1994).

Phillips-Matz, Mary Jane, *Verdi. A Biography*, (Oxford, New York: 1993).

Rosenthal, Harold and Warrack, John (eds) *The Concise Oxford History of Opera* (Oxford: 1980).

Rosselli, John, *Music and Musicians in 19th-Century Italy* (London: 1991).

Sachs, Harvey, *Toscanini* (London: 1978).

Sachs, Harvey, *Reflections on Toscanini* (London: 1992).

Servadio, Gaia, *The Real Traviata* (London: 1994).

Slonimsky, Nicolas, *Lexicon of Musical Invective* (Seattle and London: 1953).

Southwell-Sander, Peter, *Verdi: His Life and Times* (Tunbridge Wells: 1978).

Swanston, Hamish E G, *In Defence of Opera* (London: 1978).

Toye, Francis, *Verdi: Lives of the Great Composers* (ed A L Bacharach), (London: 1943).

Walker, Frank, *The Man Verdi* (London: 1962).

Weaver, William (ed), *Verdi. A documentary* (Berlin: 1980).

Werfel, Franz, *Verdi, A Novel of the Opera* (New York: 1947).

Whittall, Arnold, Romantic Music (London: 1987).

Williams, Stephen, *Come to the Opera* (London: 1948).

Picture Sources

The author and publishers wish to express their thanks to the following sources of illustrative material and/or permission to reproduce it. They will make proper acknowledgements in future editions in the event that any omissions have occurred.

The Lebrecht Music Collection: pp. iii, xiv, 6, 8, 30, 35, 40, 56, 60, 63, 73, 77, 86, 89, 94, 105, 109, 111, 128, 145, 147; Barbara Meier, Dortmund: pp. 2, 68, 96; La Scala, Milan: pp. 11, 12, 22, 135; Alberto Carrara Verdi: pp. 29, 64, 81, 83, 119, 134; Knesebeck Verlag: pp. 55, 122; Ricordi & Co, Milan: p. 143; Dalmazio Archive, Busseto: p. 47; Giancarlo Costa: p. 58.

Index

lives in Paris, 46; relationship with Giuseppina Strepponi, x–xi, 46, 47–8, 50, 69; breaks with his parents, 50; life at Sant'Agata, 56–8, 68, 94–5, 121, 144; decorations, 62, 89, 93, 120, 143; biographies of, 62–3; religion and attitude to clergy, 63, 115; friendships, 76–7, 118; letter-writing style, 78; artistic principles, 79; marries Giuseppina Strepponi, 85; and politics, ix–x, 86–7, 100; made honorary member of Academie Française, 87; visit to Russia, 88–9; and Manzoni, 101, 115; and Rossini memorial, 102; depression, 110, 118, 126; composes string quartet, 112; relationship with Teresa Stolz, xi, 112–15, 146; autobiography, 120, 141; annual routine, 121–2; 'musical Round Table', 122; views on music, 124–5, 144; exhaustion, 126, 142; consciousness of age, 135, 142; suffers stroke, 144; death, 146

WORKS: *Aida*, 78, 104–10, 111, 114, 115, 116, 117, 122, 128, 140; *Alzira*, 27, 28, 30; *Aroldo*, 76–7; *L'assedio di Arlem*, 32; *Attila*, 27, 28, 29, 37; *Ave Maria*, 120, 133, 143; *Un ballo in maschera*, 80–84, 91, 108, 111, 140; *La battaglia di Legnano*, 27, 32, 44–5; *Il corsaro*, 28, 30, 31; *I deliri di Saul*, 11; *Don Carlos*, 93, 97–101, 103, 107, 108, 115, 116, 124, 140; *I due Foscari*, 27, 30, 31, 32, 39; *Ernani*, 22, 27, 29, 31, 32, 35, 43, 81, 90, 121; *Falstaff*, 7, 133, 135–42, 143; *La forza del destino*, ix, 88–91, 104, 113; *Gerusalemme*, 50; *Un giorno di regno*, 15–16; *Giovanna d'Arco*, 27, 30, 38, 40; *Jérusalem*, 30, 41–2, 46; *I Lombardi alla prima crociata*, 25, 26, 30, 31, 32; *Luisa Miller*, 48–9, 58; *Macbeth*, 35–9, 58, 92, 99; *I masnadieri*, 27, 28, 40–41, 129; *Nabucco*, ix, 18–22, 25, 26, 28, 31, 61;

Oberto, Conte di San Bonifacio, 13–15, 21, 78; *Otello*, 116, 117, 121, 123, 126–32, 133, 140–41; *Pater Noster*, 120; *Pietà Signor*, 145; *Quattro pezzi sacri*, 143, 146; *Re Lear*, 78–9, 123; *Requiem*, 114, 115–18, 119, 120, 141; *Rigoletto*, vii, xii, 27, 51–4, 56, 61, 68, 74, 90, 95, 103, 116; *Simon Boccanegra*, 76, 80, 108, 123; *Stiffelio*, 51, 75, 76; *La traviata*, 63, 65–9, 116; *Le Trouvère*, 75; *Il trovatore*, 56, 59–62, 68; *Les Vêpres siciliennes*, 41, 58, 61, 71–5, 97, 107

Verdi, Giuseppina, *see* Strepponi, Giuseppina
Verdi, Icilio Romano, 10; death, 16
Verdi, Luigia (née Uttini), 1; death, 50
Verdi, Virginia, 10; death, 12
verismo, 125; operas, 144
Victor Emmanuel II, King, 42, 43, 86–7; biography, 43
Victoria, Queen, 40
Vidalenza, 50
Vienna, 132
Villafranca, Treaty of, 85
Villanova d'Arda, 56, 125, 135, 144
von Bülow, Cosima, 62
von Bülow, Hans, 117

Wagner, Richard, viii, 37, 62, 77, 79, 99, 103, 123; biography, 62; influence in Italy, 93, 110–11; *Lohengrin*, 102, 109, 111; *Die Meistersinger von Nürnberg*, 102, 124, 138; *Parsifal*, 124; *Tannhäuser*, 93; *Tristan und Isolde*, 97, 111
Waldmann, Maria, 109, 116, 118, 136
Weber, Carl Maria von, 41; biography, 37; *Der Freischütz*, 36
Wilhelm I, King, 106
Wolf-Ferrari, Ermanno, 140, 143

Young Italy movement, 23